P25√/s

EARLY VICTORIAN SPITTAL
(1837 – 1864)

Michael Cullen

Including extracts from
'Spittal and Spittal Folks' by George Russell Jackson
first published around 1873

FOR MOTHER AND FATHER

ISBN 0 9549474 0 1
Design by www.simprimstudio.com
Printed and bound in Great Britain by Martins the Printers Limited, Berwick-upon-Tweed
www.martins-the-printers.com

Published by Michael Cullen in 2005

Introduction

The dates chosen to start and finish are of course rather arbitrary, especially the second. One can though perhaps reasonably come to a halt during the comparatively uneventful mid-1860's. The chapter titled 'The Village' goes back a bit further to take in aspects of Spittal's earlier colourful past and there are occasional references to later events. Some sections outline the Berwick background.

Concentration on a restricted period sharpens the focus in a way that would not be possible in a volume of similar size spanning the centuries. It was too a time of rich variety. It saw the end of whaling but the coming of steamers and the railway; the continued growth of the herring fishing and the establishment of the Foundry, Forge, Chemical Works, and Manure factories; there was the learning of the new Subscription School and the annual uproar of the Feast.

A group of family names predominates throughout this period. I have shown a family link where this has been clear and relevant but attempted no more. To do so would require a different intention and knowledge base. Here though it might be made clear that George Carr, businessman, and George Carr, Spittal innkeeper and fisherman, were different people. Both had on on occasion to be distinguished from other George Carrs.

This account ends when photography was in its early stages thus limiting pictorial possibilities. Its sequel, 'Later Victorian Spittal', will though be able to make full use of the abundant photography of this period. Here the frequent quotations, mostly from the *Berwick Advertiser* and the *Berwick Journal,* are included to give a verbal feel of the times.

Contents

..... And Going

Growing Up In 1850's Spittal

Maps And Illustrations

Acknowledgments

The following items are reproduced by permission of Berwick Record Office:
Board of Health Map, 1852, (U. 10/4); Map of *'The Proposed Railway from Greenwich Colliery to Berwick Bridge'*, 1843, (T.3/1); a poster advertising the ordination of the Rev. William Porteous, 1850, (BRO.6); and verses from the anonymous *'Ballad of the Waterworks'*, c.1858, (G.29/21); also for material relating to the *Norfolk* from *'Spittal News'* (B.R.O 695)

Fife Council Museums: Kirkcaldy Museum and Art Gallery have given permission for the reproduction of the photograph of the whaler, the *Lord Gambier* at Kirkcaldy Harbour.

Berwick Borough Museum supplied the copy of the 1856 painting of the 1848 wooden railway bridge over The Tweed.
Birlinn Ltd permitted the passage by the Rev. William Whitehouse quoted by Raymond Lamont-Brown in his *'The Life and Times of Berwick-upon-Tweed'*.
Neil and Sue's Picture Framing supplied the section of the Tweed map and photographs of the Red Lion and Commercial Inns.
Paul Angus loaned the Red Lion logo.

Particular thanks to **Tony Langmack** for taking the trouble to read an earlier draft of this text. Thanks too to **Willie Heckles** for generous disposal of his local knowledge.

Sources

Of the books and other printed sources consulted the following have been referred to and at times quoted from:

The History of Berwick-upon-Tweed by Dr. John Fuller (1799)
Rambles in Northumberland by Stephen Oliver (1835)
Mieldenvold the Student by Frederick Sheldon (1843)
History of Berwick-upon-Tweed by Frederick Sheldon (1849)
The Ballad of the Waterworks (anon. circa 1858)
The Life of James Redpath by Charles F. Horner (1926)
Spittal Past and Present by Frank Swinney (1966)
The Life and Times of Berwick-upon-Tweed by Raymond Lamont-Brown (1988)

1 A stranger's boast

In the early summer of 1838 a stranger arrived in Spittal to work on a building site. He was Alexander McDougle, forty-one years old, five feet eight inches in height, and fair-haired. He said he was from the Highlands of Scotland but was generally thought to be Irish.

He was entertaining company, a man who liked a few drinks and who enlivened the working hours by recounting stories of his many escapes from gaol. He was about to add another.

*   *   *   *   *   *   *

What he'd been up to emerged at the Quarter Sessions of July 8th. While walking past the Berwick house of the Denovan's he'd spotted a peacock in the garden and sensed a business opportunity. Grabbing it, he carried it off to Berwick Fair where he offered it to Thomas Douglas, a fireman on the steamer *Manchester,* for seven shillings. Douglas accepted it with some misgiving as he asked McDougle in Spanish whether or not it had been stolen. He then took it to The London and Berwick Tavern where he asked Mrs Turner to look after it for him until the *Manchester* sailed, his idea being to sell it in London. Unfortunately for both of them a servant of the Denovan's, Robert Thompson, went out for a drink at that tavern the same evening, recognised the bird, and took it home.

In court McDougle resorted to blustering defiance, denying 'with great vehemence' that the bird which had been brought into court and now stood displayed before them was the same bird. Asked how he could be sure it was the Denovan's bird Chief Police Officer Proudfoot said he was able to recognise it from a mark he'd made on its leg, a typical ploy by an officer with a strong detective record. Peacocks had been stolen before. Other witnesses concurred with Proudfoot.

There was more. Nine black and white fowls had disappeared from the Denovan's garden at the same time and McDougle was charged with the theft of one of these.

And more. A tub had been removed from outside the house of Mr. Paulin, a shoemaker. This had been sold to a shopkeeper for sixpence before being surrendered to Proudfoot.

Questioned in court, Mr. Paulin claimed to have recognised McDougle's voice outside his house which brought this retort. *"How do you know my voice? I'm in the habit of speaking Spanish when I'm drunk."* When questioned he asserted, *"I did not steal the tub. I was drunk that morning, and sold it again to Catherine Waite."*

This farrago of a defence cut little ice with the jury who without retiring found him guilty of stealing both the birds and the tub or with the Recorder who sentenced him to two consecutive periods of four months hard labour. In the event the gaol was to contain him for less than three weeks.

*   *   *   *   *   *   *

Berwick magistrates had been warned a few years previously of the inadequacy of the Town Hall gaol and threatened with the loss of the Quarter Sessions if a new gaol was not built. There was a good deal of discussion but less action and no new gaol until 1850. McDougle was sent to the Town Hall.

The prison reformer Elizabeth Fry had criticised Berwick Gaol for failing to provide the prisoners with any form of constructive occupation. Since then teasing oakum had been introduced. This was not in the same league as Morpeth which had moved on to the production of manufactured articles but McDougle saw an opportunity with oakum - that of producing a new rope from the frayed and tattered strands of old ones.

This he did, and managed to conceal the completed rope in an upper chamber. The other part of his plan was to recover his greatcoat, then in pawn. He persuaded the gaoler to lend him a shilling to redeem it and then to allow him to spread it on the roof to dry.

On the damp morning of July 26th the prisoners routinely worked the oakum which was then taken on to the roof to dry. When it started to rain the gaoler asked McDougle to go and bring it inside. This was the moment he had been waiting for.

Having climbed through the trap-hole he slammed the door securely down with a force unnecessary for his assigned task, gathered the concealed rope and took it out onto the leads where he seized his greatcoat. One end of the rope he fastened to a railing then, using his greatcoat to mask the friction, he slid the fifty-odd feet to the ground. He then donned the greatcoat, largely hiding the prison uniform of blue jacket, waistcoat, and trousers, and made off.

The rain had driven most people indoors and his dramatic descent was witnessed only by a boy, playing nearby. He rang the prison bell and told the gaoler what he'd seen. The gaoler alerted the police and some constables set out after him but returned empty-handed about one o'clock in the morning.

The gaoler, who seems to have been a mightily obliging fellow, reckoned the escape must have taken no more than three minutes.

The rope was found to be half an inch thick. So McDougle vanished, but must have been remembered in Spittal for many a year.

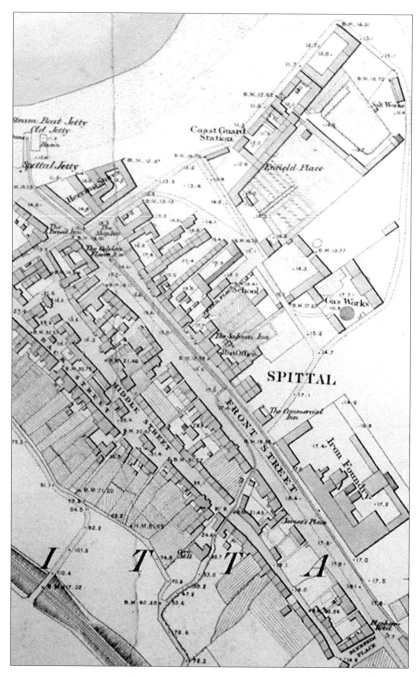

Spittal North End. Board of Health Map 1852

2 Spittal village

Spittal had been much in need of the building work on which McDougle had been briefly engaged. Dr. Fuller, writing in his 1799 History of Berwick-upon-Tweed, found the prospect grim. *'Excepting some houses which have been built of late years, the buildings of this populous village are intolerably bad, which frequently must become a source of disease to its many inhabitants..'* The writer of the entry for the 1827 Directory described much the same scene. *'Many of the old houses are in a decayed condition but several new buildings have been erected.'* The visitor's eye seemingly sought relief in the new building from the general feel of run-down decrepitude.

'It consists of two streets, one of which is wide and the other very narrow,' noted the same directory. Main Street had two distinctive features; a railway that had been lain to carry stone from Hud's Head to the jetty for the building of the pier but which was then being used for coal and a whiffy burn that aroused comment. *'If that filthy burn which runs through the principal street was covered in and the inhabitants prevented from throwing out their ashes and other dirt before their doors, a great addition would be made to the comfort of the visitors as well as of the inhabitants themselves.'* There was an all-pervading *'ancient fish-like smell'* and pigs and other livestock were often seen in the streets.

*   *   *   *   *   *   *

Two developments separated by about fifty years greatly altered the look of Spittal. The first was the enclosure in 1800 of the Common which stretched south from the settled part of the village to Hud's Head. This had a twofold effect. The enclosed area was *'excellent land and well-fenced.... which advances.... property to twice the value it was formerly'*. At the same time the *'vagabonds and smugglers'* who had used it as *'their lurking place'* were driven away. With their limited capacity for concealing either themselves or goods most of these were probably small-time operators and general nuisances. The second great change was the making of the embankment to carry the Newcastle line to the Royal Border Bridge which gave the village a mighty earthen backdrop.

The pattern of settlement at the northern end of the village as established by 1800 was much the same as today's and can be seen detailed in the Board of Health's 1852 map. A fairly continuous line of houses ran south as far as today's Commercial Road on the east side and Blenheim Place on the west. There was a line of about a dozen properties beyond this on the east side of Main Street and a cluster of bathing houses nearer the coast but houses at the south end were otherwise few and scattered. Most of this area was field and garden as it was too behind Back Street.

Much of the land to the east of Main Street consisted of Common,waste land, and sea banks. Here owners' rights were less visibly defined and sometimes needed legal reinforcement. A sizeable stretch had been given to Greenwich Hospital after the Crown's confiscation of the estate of the Third Earl of Derwentwater when the collapse of the 1715 Jacobite rising led to his capture and execution. Houses on Greenwich land were required to pay a door tax, something that persisted until 1925. On the death of William Fair in 1848 a Press notice warned against the taking of sand from the links without the permission of the heirs of the estate.

There were grey areas. While parts of this area were treated as Common Land legal rights were occasionally exercised. Robert Boston observed in the 1870's that there had been much discussion about land rights in Spittal. Talk became action in 1881 when John Burn enclosed some land by Sea Road provoking meetings, rackety demonstrations, the burning of at least four effigies, and a Newcastle court case.

East of Main Street too lay most of Spittal's working parts. The Iron Foundry and Gas Company appeared during the early Victorian period while the Herring Yards were by then well-established. There was also a salt mill on the Point. Here too were reminders of Spittal's colourful past.

         *   *   *   *   *   *   *

It was said of Eyemouth during its smuggling heyday that there was more of it below ground than above. Spittal too had substantial underground chambers with tunnels running out to the links. By the Victorian period these had become mere curiosities, an intriguing spectacle for the summer visitors.

A number of distinctive features were later found in various properties. The Bell Inn had a concealed cavity under the hearthstone. When number 9, Main Street, was being demolished a hiding hole was found in the kitchen and a recess covered with loose stones was discovered to contain parchment labels. This suggests organised trafficking of the kind that is known to have existed: there was,for example, a going rate of fifteen shillings for taking a box or bale from the Solway to Edinburgh. Upstairs in the same house panels could be slid out to gain entry to a room. Number 15, Main Street, *'The Cottage of the Blue Step'*, contained a smugglers' hole under the stone slab which formed the step at the back door. This was about the size of a box bed. According to Frederick Sheldon, writing in 1849, there was considerable evidence of past activity.

> *'The old spirit of smuggling has now deserted it and the present revenue guard look uninterestedly at the vast underground receptacles and secret hiding places in which the fishermen and smugglers of the last century stowed away their cargoes.'*

It had been very different in the days when smugglers and the excise sought to get the better of each other. Speed and concealment were necessary conditions for successful smuggling.

> *'In the old smuggling and buccaneering times it was a great place for landing contraband articles. On a dark night, at a given signal, the lugger stood in for the shore; her boats hoisted out and her whole cargo landed on the Point of Spittal; brawny men would dash into the surf, and in twenty minutes not a keg or bale would be seen'.*

The cheapness of some articles is evidence of their profusion. George Jackson mentions the habit fishermen had once had of taking gin with their breakfast. Another voice described nocturnal treats.

> *'Gin and brandy could be obtained for a trifle and a yard of tobacco for a penny. When a lugger appeared it was said 'the cow had calved'. It was a common occurrence to have a kilderkin of gin or brandy left at your door in the dead of night.'*

Goods from the luggers which at one time were very frequent were taken as far as the Cheviots.

This sea-borne trade continued on a reduced scale after it had died out in Spittal as occasional interceptions show. Its extinction in Spittal was almost certainly the result of placing a substantial coastguard establishment, station and a row of cottages, along Sandstell Road. Until transferred to the Admiralty in 1856 the coastguards were a branch of the excise. Little was now going to escape their notice.

A different form of smuggling did though continue with much illicit whisky passing through the Paxton, Lamberton, and Mordington tolls.

> *'Many bladders full of whisky have been carried by the stalwart*

fish-wives from the tolls into the town, to make the burgesses merry with stolen licquor.'

No doubt it added to the jollity of life but it was a different matter if you got caught carrying it. In 1839 one Dorothy Ferguson was fined twenty-five pounds *'for carrying spirits without a licence'*. On other occasions the same penalty was imposed for *'removing two bottles of whisky from Scotland to England'*, *'smuggling a grey-beard containing one gallon of whisky'*, and being caught with *'three and a half gallons of British spirits'*.

There were plenty of suppliers. There were many traders along the Scottish side of the border, from Coldstream to Langholm, whose stocks of whisky clearly exceeded the capacity of the local community and who made unobtrusive nightly trips to England. Whisky was then far more popular in Northumberland than in England as a whole where it was second-best to gin. The volume of the smuggled trade depended much on the excise differential which varied over the years from over nine shillings to about one shilling and sixpence. Stephen Oliver, writing in 1835, thought the then differential of four shillings an insufficient incentive and responsible for *'the very depressed state of the trade'*.

The other constraint was of course the excise. By 1834 there were fifty-six officers strategically placed along the Eastern Border with co-ordination provided by Riding Officers. Besides the four coastguards placed in their midst Spittalers would also have been aware of the revenue cutter, *Mermaid*, hovering in the background.

Most of those caught seem to have been small-time operators.Such a fuss was made of a more substantial case in 1838 as to suggest that it was quite exceptional. Seven publicans, four from Berwick and three from Tweedmouth, connived at smuggling into Berwick a quantity of spirits under cover of the Lamberton Races. The spirit was placed in carts and covered with tents and other paraphernalia.The excise though got wind of the wheeze for on their return each publican found an excise officer stationed outside his house. A special Magistrates Court was convened at which all the excise officers were present. Six of them got the usual twenty-five pound fine while a seventh was freed for lack of evidence.

Excise successes seemed to show that serious traffickers were now giving Berwick and Spittal a wide berth. In March 1847 1,100 lbs.of tobacco carried in two hogsheads was uncovered on the road to Alnwick. Two years later the French cutter *Le Comte* was boarded off Fast Castle and its captain charged with intent to smuggle twenty bales of tobacco. The law now had a long reach. The vessels *Emma* and *Tullymet* must have thought themselves fairly safe swapping coal for brandy in the lee of the Fame Islands until the *Mermaid* appeared and charged both captains.

More subdued though Spittal was than it had been smuggling, or the suspicion of it, was the cause of a tragic incident. Trying to escape a coastguard James Beveridge attempted to hide behind a bush by the Billendean Road where he was shot dead. In the wake of fierce protests that he'd not been involved in smuggling the officer concerned vanished and the coastguards were disarmed. A cross inscribed on one of the railway arches was said to have been visible within living memory.

*   *   *   *   *   *   *

Counterfeiting and forging were other ways of cheating the revenue and were widely practised in the early years of the century. Skill levels varied from the expertise of a London forger able to copy signatures and transact business in someone else's name with such conviction that the victim often subsequently had the greatest difficulty in telling apart genuine and fraudulent acts to the often more amateurish efforts in the Borough.

The discovery of a family enterprise in Walkergate in 1816 led to the charge against John Johnson of *'feloniously colouring with materials producing the colour of silver a piece of based coin – resembling a sixpence'.* A coin had been put to the test by sending a boy and girl into a shop for a pot of whisky. It worked once but when tried again Ann Wilson, wife of the spirit dealer, *'thinking it not a good piece took back the tea-cup and the whiskey'.* As they were all illiterate they may have had problems with the lettering.

In June 1820 Thomas Hope, Constable, chanced on what seems to have been a more proficient operation. Looking for some persons charged with theft in the Magdalen Fields he saw three men running and overtook and stopped a man carrying a large parcel. Parcels often invited suspicion. Taken into custody two other packages were found in his trouser pockets, the whole amounting to thirty-four pounds, ten shillings, and sixpence.

Spittal too had a colourful cast of semi-mythical characters. Bobby the Barber occupied a *'little house'* in Main Street which had a secret outlet to the links. It was known as *'The Coiner's Den'.* His practice was to take the counterfeit money to London to dispose of but on his last journey up Billendean he was arrested and later hanged. This was supposed to have happened about 1800.

A large quantity of coins was unearthed in May 1886 in Sea Road while a trench was being laid for gas pipes. The horde contained Spanish and English coins dating from 1670, among them crowns and half-crowns from the time of Queen Anne, George IV, and William IV. An elderly inhabitant thought the coins *'purloined'* from foreign seamen by Sam Bell, whatever that meant. He was a man with a reputation as his house was regularly searched by law officers. A later account described him as a coiner and drunkard, a man who sold much of his property when *'in his cups'*. Both accounts end with his being tried and hanged in Edinburgh.

The most intriguing of the smugglers and counterfeiters was Richard Mendham, whose activities provided Sir Walter Scott with some source material while he was writing 'Redgauntlet' as he described.

> *'About twenty years ago there was along the frontier an organised gang of coiners, forgers, and smugglers whose operations were conducted on a scale not inferior to what is here described. The chief of the party was one Richard Mendham, a carpenter, who rose to opulence. But he found a short cut to wealth, and had taken singular means for conducting his operations. Amongst these he found means to build in a suburb of Berwick called Spittal a street of small houses, as if for the investment of property. He himself inhabited one of these; another, a species of public house, was open to his confederates, who held secret and unsuspected communication with him by crossing the roofs of the intervening houses, and descending by a trap-stair which admitted them into the alcove of the dining room of Dick Mendham's private mansion. A vault, too, beneath Mendham's stable, was accessible in the manner mentioned in the novel. The post of one of the stalls turned round on a bolt being withdrawn and gave admittance to a subterranean place of concealment for contraband.'*

When first arrested Mendham was acquitted *'by want of proof and the ingenuity of his counsel'*. The second time though there was to be no reprieve and he was tried and executed at Jedburgh.

Some counterfeiting was still going on in the early years of Victoria's reign. In October 1839 one Alexander Richelton, described as *'late of Spittal'* was caught *'uttering false coin'*.

By this time Spittal had become a generally law-abiding place. In popular perception it was now less *'the haunt of nautical desperadoes'* and more *'a modest watering place'*. In May 1837 it was noted that there was *'only one man in gaol for smuggling'* and that *'the latter offence has almost ceased to exist in the Borough'.*

        *   *   *   *   *   *   *

There was a general hope that cholera, that recurrent threat, would also cease to exist. At a time when The Lancet could do no better than pose a series of questions on the cause and nature of the disease various theories were put forward. Some thought it contagious, others that it was transmitted through the atmosphere. The idea of a *'disordered atmosphere'* in which there was imbalance, rather as a medieval doctor ascribed illness to a surfeit or lack of one of the four bodily humours, was proposed as the most probable cause by the *Berwick Advertiser*. It was more specific, thinking an excess of electricity in the atmosphere the fatal ingredient. To this end it recommended the wearing of silk or other non-conductive clothes and suggested the stationing of a balloon over Berwick with a cable to draw off the surplus.

Most advice though concerned hygiene and sanitation, the lack of which were seen as facilitating the spread of the disease. One should keep rooms clean, ensure fresh air, beware unboiled water, *'tainted'* food, excessive fatigue or damp, and avoid intemperate habits, especially heavy drinking. For *'the dissipated and the dirty have been the usual victims'.*

This advice became insistent during the nation-wide outbreak of 1832. Press reports of large numbers of deaths in Glasgow, Edinburgh, and Newcastle suggested that Berwick would be lucky to escape.Periodic declines raised hopes that the outbreak was over but eventually there was a virulent outbreak, two hundred and eight cases resulting in a hundred deaths, a single November week carrying off ten Spittalers. Nor was it merely the dissolute who perished. In many towns large numbers of *'respectable persons'* had perished.|

A thirty-man Board of Health was appointed, a Soup Kitchen set up and subscriptions invited to pay for coals, food, and clothes. A physician, Dr. Grant, was engaged to help cope. The interest in his report on Spittal lies in its detailed observation.

He was shocked by the state of the streets. Main Street was in 'the filthiest state possible' it being a repository for *'filth of all kinds'*. There was too the detritus of fishing, *'effluvia arising from the putrid offal of fish'* which he found *'highly offensive and disgusting'*. This stink *'contrives to make that which was bad enough before much worse'.*

Inside the houses he found a rude simplicity. Most people *'lack the common necessaries of life'*. He found a want *'of every comfort, little or no furniture, perhaps one or two box beds, with some straw and even that not of the cleanest'.* Glass windows were unusual. For *'if there is a window in the house instead of glass its place is supplied during the day with what is perhaps used at night as a covering for their children'.*

House-room was often shared with animals. *'The pig seems sometimes to dispute for precedence in the house with the children for frequently have I seen them asleep within a few yards of each other.'* Yet having established that the village pitmen earned only twenty-one to twenty-four shillings a week he appreciated there were limits to what could be done. This though in his eyes made the presence of inns and beer-shops, *'those haunts of vice'* all the more reprehensible.

In one case outrage prompted him to name and shame. Called to attend a nine-year-old girl he provided his remedy. *'Brandy was ordered and about three or four wine glasses sent to the house and ordered to be taken at stated times.'* Then, *'having again occasion to visit her during the night, I found her cold and fast sinking...... and the man lying drunk in bed, instead of the patient getting the brandy, he had taken it..... This man was Thomas Crowther.'* (heavily underlined)

More will be heard of Thomas Crowther, cooper, whaler, herring curer, innkeeper, and Town Councillor.

✳   ✳   ✳   ✳   ✳   ✳   ✳

Legislation, local and national, attempted to clean up the streets. A bye-law of 1838 made the cleanliness of pavements and confinement of swine obligatory. Ten years later the Mayor, Dr. Henry Clarke, who'd been elected a Middle Ward Councillor by the margin of thirteen votes to six (much apathy then too) saw urban hygiene as a matter of high priority and pushed for the speedy implementation of the Health of Towns Act. Confined or not there was an abundance of pigs, chicken, and ducks. Middle Street was often called Duck Street.

A number of people fell foul of attempts to clean up the streets. Peter Knox was fined for *'allowing swine to go at large in Spittal'* while John Smith's offence was described in unusual detail. He *'did lay the contents of a certain privy at a certain street or lane there situate called Tweed Place without thoroughly removing the same before nine o'clock in the morning.... and did slop and spill such contents in the Sandstell Road in Spittal'.* Foul yards could cause friction. The shoemaker, Archibald Service's objections to the filthy state of his neighbour John Banks' yard led to wrestling between the two and to an order from the magistrates to get it cleaned up. The law could reach indoors too. Peter Richardson, a carter, was in trouble with the Inspector of Nuisances for keeping a horse in his house.

Many wanted some lighting at night. In February 1847 a public meeting in the Subscription School petitioned the Town Council for street lighting, wanting it charged to the rates. A counter-petition from thirty-nine ratepayers however argued that as there were only fifty general ratepayers in Spittal the cost would be *'oppressive'*. The Town Clerk though was of the opinion that all but two of the names on the second list had been written by the same person. Spittal was eventually lit in 1852.

*   *   *   *   *   *   *

In order to see what would be required to implement the Health of Towns Act the Town Council asked an engineer, Richard Rawlinson, to survey the Borough. His report contained the bizarre suggestion, fortunately ignored, that all or part of the Walls should be demolished in the interest of urban hygiene and expansion. Elsewhere in Berwick he came across grotesquely overcrowded buildings (several instances of more than twenty to a room), foul yards and middens and poor roads. He wanted paving and flagging of courts and yards, fuller use of slaughter-houses, better ventilation, and, above all, an improved sewerage and water system.

The section dealing with Spittal was brief but prompted protest. Rawlinson argued that Spittal's prime need was for an adequate system of sewerage and drainage. In a second report he deemed Spittal's water supply inadequate. He'd commented too on the tendency for refuse to end up in the lower parts of the village and on the irregular collection of manure. Too often farmers left it *'till it suits their convenience to take it away'* and he asked why Berwick, unlike other towns, had not made a single contractual agreement for the export of its manure.

It was Rawlinson's recommendations for a proper system of drainage and an improved water supply that caused the fuss. A public meeting of Spittal and Tweedmouth residents, for whom the same remedies had been proposed, was held and a letter of protest subsequently drafted by the herring curer and innkeeper, Thomas Crowther.

The alleged inadequacy of Spittal's water supply was hotly denied. On the contrary it was asserted that the piped supply introduced by John Miller Dickson saw an excess capacity of some seven hundred gallons running to waste each day. The drainage scheme was objected to as draining such a predominantly level area would be extremely expensive. In addition it was stated that men were employed to clean the streets four or five days a week: that the mortality figures had been grossly inflated by the presence of some two thousand railway workers: and that if improvement was needed, residents were quite capable of devising the means. The Town Council, which doubled as the local Board of Health, was seen as a body with a record of *expensive mismanagement* in which they could place no confidence.

Crowther and Rawlinson expressed directly contrary views over Spittal's water supply. Crowther seems the more credible as it's hard to see how he, on behalf of fellow protesters, could have claimed a surplus of good quality water had that not been the case. Indeed, Berwick's water was the real problem. In 1846 the Mayor had said it was no better than mud being *'in such a filthy state as to be literally unfit for human use'*. The supply of this dubious liquid was also scanty, the pipes being dry for hours.

It looks rather as though Rawlinson, who was in favour of a single Water Board having control over all works in the Borough was rather adjusting the facts to fit his theory that bigger would mean better. He subsequently directed the construction of the New Farm Waterworks, a flawed undertaking that saw his reputation slump from that of *'eminent engineer'* to the laughing stock satirically lampooned in *'The Ballad of the Waterworks'*. At first all had seemed in order.

> *The water ran, the water sprang,*
> *Fed by the genial rains,*
> *Till every household was supplied,*
> *And flush'd were all the drains.*
>
> *From every closet copious streams*
> *Ran to the river down;*
> *And not a particle of filth*
> *Was left in all the town.*

An analysis though showed the water to be of poor quality. But at least there was plenty of it - or was there.

> *They went again to view the work,*
> *As they had done before;*
> *And ruefully they look'd upon*
> *The New Farm Reservoir.*

They saw a vast expanse of mud,
Dried by the solar beam,
Through which there ran, in devious course,
A tiny, thread-like stream.

The Board of Health saw little scope for action.

And when th'inhabitants complained –
In speech as soft as honey,
They told them they could do no more,
Because they had no money.'

Not till the mid-1870's was any substantial improvement made in the quality of Berwick's water which Dr. McLagan thought the cause of many stomach disorders.

   * * * * * * *

The building work of the 1830's had made a difference. Comment tended to be more neutral or even approving. In 1840 a contrast was being drawn between *'this once destitute and neglected village and its present interesting and improving appearance'* by a reporter who seemed in rather a mellow mood after attending the first and highly satisfactory examination at the new school. Frederick Sheldon described *'an irregular cluster of houses of all shapes and sizes, the better sort sprung lately into existence'.*

In 1845 John Burn advertised properties for sale. These were *'two new self-contained houses.... consisting of kitchen, parlour, bed room and bed closet and a piece of ground connected therewith suitable for building on'.* Situated near the new schoolhouse, these sound highly desirable.

In fact though more was demolished than built during the 1840's as the following figures show.

	1841	1851
Population	1,631	1,746
Inhabited Houses	261	233
Uninhabited Houses	32	12
Building	1	1
Average no. of people per house	6.25	7.50

While the population increased by one hundred and fifteen during this decade there were twenty-eight fewer houses. In all nearly fifty inhabited and uninhabited houses disappeared during this decade, suggesting a good deal of terminal decay.

In 1854 concern was expressed in the Manor Court of Tweedmouth and Spittal about the dangerous state of some Spittal buildings. One indeed had recently collapsed. A jury went on a tour of inspection unappreciated by the local residents whose hostility was expressed *'in a manner locally characteristic'*. The Town Council found *'some in ruins..... others in a state of extreme dilapidation'*. Yet as Councillor Ramsey pointed out censure alone would do little good if the occupants of derelict properties lacked the money to repair them. The Works Committee was asked to investigate and report. When called for though the report had not been written and seemingly never was. This was not the only occasion on which such follow-up work was neglected, an indication that Spittal's affairs did not rate too highly on the Council's scale of priorities.

Occasionally a light was shone into a murky corner. The four deaths from cholera in the Elliott household in 1848 were largely ascribed to the insanitary state of their house and stretch of Back Street. Then when the eighty-four-year old Margaret Chisholm fell to her death from an unrailed outer staircase there was disquiet over the squalor in which she'd been found to have been living. While there had been pleasing recent building a number of black spots remained. The north end was badly decayed with a row of four derelict houses just south of the crossroads.

Many of the older houses were later found to have exceedingly thick walls as though built as a refuge from perhaps the excise or the Press Gang, often on the lookout for strong young fishermen. Stone could be obtained from The Old Quarry. Tradition had it that a man could take for house-building as much as he could carry.

Only a minority of mainly better-off families had a house to themselves. In 1831 Berwick's 2,118 families lived in 1,190 houses and Newcastle figures show an almost identical proportion of just under two families to a house. A person's abode might be described as *'a room in a house in Back Street'*. Even Chief Police Officer Proudfoot, a married man with family, had to make do with two rooms in Marygate.

* * * * * * *

During the late 1840's gangs of often unruly men roamed Spittal's streets. These were some of the two thousand odd navvies then engaged on construction of the Newcastle railway line. There were frequently large numbers of them near Brighton House.

This was the site of a tommy shop put there by the contractors which the men were often obliged to use. They were paid monthly which left a recurring need for cash, or a cash substitute, before the month was up:in part because they were paid only for three weeks, the fourth week's pay being retained to ensure the men's continued work.

The monopolistic profiteering involved in the truck system, already outlawed in shops, raised the ire of the *Berwick Advertiser*. *'The large body of workers residing in Spittal are in a state of bondage and thraldom,'* it commented. Resentment at this treatment may have been behind some of the disturbances. Spittal residents complained of night plunder by *'midnight marauders'*. Blackstock and Mackay, the main contractors, had problems with site security. They out-drank the workers on the Edinburgh line who *'might be seen drunk an entire day, but not continuously drunk for a whole week at a time'*. A policeman was stationed in Spittal to keep an eye on them and a lock-up considered though not built. In the summer Of 1846 there were complaints of riotous behaviour in Berwick, where they preferred drinking, and the policeman was sent back to Berwick. Spittal workers don't though seem to have taken part in the biggest commotion of the time, the Railway Riots of 1847, which occupied the Magistrates Courts for some weeks.

Meanwhile in their soberer working hours the navvies were radically transforming the physical landscape of Spittal and Tweedmouth with the creation of the embankments that were to carry the line. There were *'huge forests of scaffolding, raised to an immense height'* with *'innumerable carts, wheelbarrows, and other varieties of mechanical appliance'*.

Spittal residents would have noticed the stages of bridge building; the two years spent driving the piles and laying the under masonry while three steam engines pumped the coffer dams day and night; the construction of a temporary wooden bridge and its testing with increasingly strong loads; the gradual formation of the present structure with its near million and a half bricks and quarter million feet of masonry; and the appearance of the royal train as it carried Queen Victoria to the twelve-minute formal naming of the bridge.

Memorable too must have been the firework display that night. Watchers saw volleys of signal rockets, blue fire shells and dazzling cascades of stars, serpents, fountains and diamonds, lovers' knots, wheels and showers of fire. The climax of the display was *'The Royal Temple'*. High in the heavens there suddenly appeared *'revolving pyramids suspended by large ionic columns'*, bearing the initials of Her Most Gracious

The temporary wooden railway bridge over the Tweed
Built in 1848 this structure provided the link between the North British and York, Newcastle and Berwick lines before the completion of the Royal Border Bridge in 1850.

Majesty and containing the words *'God Save the Queen'* surmounted by the British Crown while *'Roman candles, a grand discharge of shells... and flights of rockets'* filled the night sky.

Later it emerged that Queen Victoria had not been altogether impressed being disappointed there had not been more water in the Tweed.

*   *   *   *   *   *   *

One man was to have a profound influence on the development of Spittal in the second half of the century. This was James T. Wilson, described in 1856 as *'a gentleman who has lately come to Spittal'*, who started up what was to become the North of England Chemical Works.

A Dundonian, he spent his younger days studying and demonstrating the science of chemistry. It was in that role that many Berwickers would have first encountered him as he gave some lectures on the properties of light at the Mechanics' Institute. These were well received. *'The lecture was a very instructive one and given in such a popular manner that it must have been understood by the meanest intelligence,'* was one opinion.

The significance of his works was that the sulphuric acid that it produced was used by the manure factories which started up on the Point. It may well have been why some owners chose to site their factories there. Speaking at The Mayor's Dinner of 1875 he reviewed development. *'He confessed, although it might appear vain, he was a little proud of those chimneys, having all risen from his own small chimney being the first.'*

In 1860 his own *'small chimney'* had been superseded by a *'beautiful and well-executed'* one of a hundred feet, the first striking landmark on the Point.

Active in the affairs of the Borough he served as a Town Councillor and did what he could on Spittal's behalf. In 1857 he joined the debate about the state of Spittal's streets. Following complaints, the Town Council decided on an inspection to see if they could be got any cleaner. Mr. Anderson, Interim Inspector of Nuisances, had a look and found Front Street as Main Street was sometimes called in a fair state but the back streets *'very indifferent'*. Mr.Wilson though took a far stronger line. He thought the *'deplorable condition'* of the streets was driving away summer visitors - he'd met one gentleman who'd told him he was never coming back. And wasn't the accumulated fetid rubbish a breeding ground for cholera? He did secure Council agreement to more regular street cleaning.

He was too one of the initial members of the Spittal Improvement Committee, a body set up as the result of a quite untypical burst of constructive empathy by the Town Council. The idea was seized with enthusiasm, projects for tree planting and seat placement being submitted and approved before Tweedmouth had got round to appointing a committee.

Before coming to Spittal he'd founded an alum works at Falkirk. Around 1870 he moved to Edinburgh, leaving his son Robert to run the Spittal factory, and started up further chemical plants at Leith, Forres, and Selkirk. The level of employment directly and indirectly produced by his works must have made him easily Spittal's most substantial industrialist.

*　　*　　*　　*　　*　　*　　*

Another business appeared in Spittal in 1855 when Thomas Black moved his Forge from Etal. This firm, founded in 1769, produced high-quality, award-winning spades and was later to become a considerable exporter. By 1860 it was already being spoken of as an *'extensive and justly celebrated spade forge'*.

By now there was a substantial and varied mix of industry in Spittal. Besides the Forge, the Foundry was back in operation, Mr.Wilson's Chemical works was supplying a Manure Factory, and there were too a Bone Mill and several Herring Yards. While fishing and mining remained the chief occupations there was an increasing range of opportunity. Indeed the vibrancy of Spittal, and of Tweedmouth too, prompted one observer to point a contrast. *'Berwick is like a tree whose trunk is rotten, while the branches, Tweedmouth and Spittal, are healthy and bearing fruit.'*

Local traders offered greater variety. In addition to the suppliers of basic needs there were now a hosier, dressmaker, hair dresser, and paper hanger. There was extensive house-building. The prospect of rent-paying tenants with steady jobs provided an incentive which had been lacking earlier. A line of sizeable tenements and houses sprang up on Sandstell Road where before there had been only scattered dwellings.

A disaster of May 1859　suggests that housing demand was outstripping adequate supply. David MacBeath, Herring Curer, had let out a house of seven or eight rooms in his yard. Fire broke out one night in a ground floor room. It was later found to have been started by *'a drunken character named William Crystal having thrown a shovelful of red-hot ashes onto his bed'*. The other inhabitants, all in bed at the time, were forced to flee for their lives leaving behind property later valued at one hundred and fifty pounds.

There was no fire-fighting equipment in Spittal and it took the Berwick engine two hours to reach the scene. In the meantime all that could be done was to protect nearby properties which included David MacBeath's own Herring premises, Henderson's Bone-Crushing Mill and a granary stored with bones. A second house was burnt but the fire spread no further.

These two houses were found to have been housing eleven families in all. No doubt this high density occupation was the reason for the timely discovery of the fire and lack of casualties. A committee was set up to raise funds for those left destitute.

∗   ∗   ∗   ∗   ∗   ∗   ∗

Along with the optimism there were complaints. By 1860 the ferry landing was *in a most shameful state*, passengers having to walk through mud at low tide. There were demands for both a police presence and a lock-up in Spittal supported by Superintendent Anderson who pointed out it cost two shillings and sixpence to take a drunk man to Berwick. This matter was deferred by the Town Council. In other words, nothing was done about it. Then, despite Mr. Wilson's efforts, the streets were once again being described as dirty and untidy. Whatever was done though Main Street would not be substantially improved until the open sewer that ran down its length was covered over at the end of the century.

Petitions were frequent. These served to give the authorities an awareness of concerns but prompted action only if they happened to strike a receptive chord. With only some two hundred on the electoral role in each of the three wards local issues could be treated with some disdain unless the protesters were persons of influence or serious disorder threatened. Yet the Council could be bullied and cowed into submission. In later years John Watt was to show how it could be done while that fine polemical journalist *'Rambler'* frequently highlighted Spittal's deficiencies and noted the stirrings of what he termed *'Home-Rulism'*. Then after Robert Boston's election to the Town Council in 1870 Spittal's needs were less easily deflected.

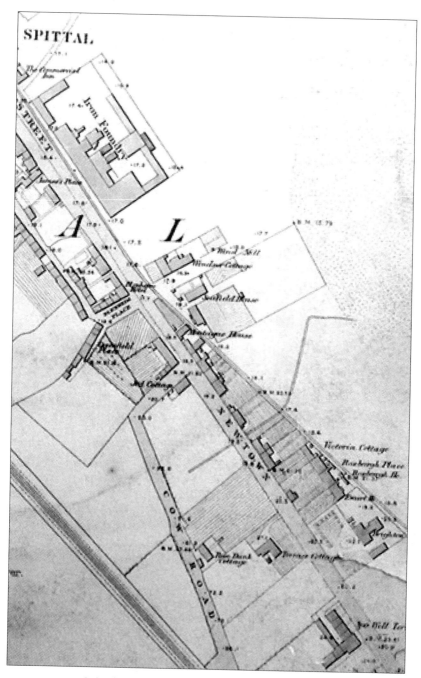

Spittal South End. Board of Health Map 1852

3 Taking the waters: The Spa

Spittal's prime attractions for summer visitors were its spa waters and beach. Taking the waters was recommended for *'Those who have been effected with a leprous or scorbutic humour in the blood'*. Large claims were made for it and it may have benefited those suffering from iron deficiency. *'It has made many cures among the poor...... nay, it has been efficacious to thousands.'*

There were other attractions. Baths, already a popular feature in the 1820's, became more elaborate. By this time it was also possible to take a trip to Holy Island. In 1838 excursions to Berwick became a more attractive prospect with the introduction of Mr. Wilson's steam ferry *Queen*. Making it possible to avoid the *'wild and stony path'* and the often exorbitant boatmen, this was better still the following year when he halved the fare to a penny. For much of the 1840's there were too the comings and goings of the Leith, Newcastle, and London steamers.

There was though one line of criticism which persisted. It was noted in 1825 that *'the accommodation which the village can furnish, and the attractions it can offer, are few when compared with places of more fashionable resort'*. It never did attract sufficient confidence and investment to break into the major resort league, to become *'The Brighton of the North'* as some optimistically hoped. But there were plenty who liked it well enough as it was. In 1838 it was reported that some families had been visiting for more than twenty-five years.

By this date the popularity of Spittal as a resort had grown to the extent that visitors had sometimes to be turned away for lack of accommodation. During the fine weather of early July 1837 Spittal was described as *'nearly full'*. *'Departures have not yet occurred; and as the coaches, which now drive into the village, are every day crowded, the quantity of respectable persons accommodated is immense.'* At the height of the season there were often three coaches a week from Kelso.

Keen to attract a sufficient share of this influx the proprietors of the lodging houses tried *'to extend and improve the accommodation for visitors, vying with each other for taste and convenience'*. Mrs Sanderson drew attention to the new stable and coach house and the *'newly papered and painted'* rooms.

The beach became sufficiently populous for a degree of order and propriety to be insisted on. During the summer of 1836 the *'admixture'* of ladies and gentlemen along its length aroused complaint. The following summer notices were posted in the village explaining the rather odd arrangement of reserving the central stretch for ladies and putting gentlemen at both ends. Two years later the rather more straightforward division of ladies at the north and gents at the south with a shield and a stake marking the boundary was adopted.

'*In summer Spittal is in its glory,*' wrote Frederick Sheldon, evocatively contemplating a summer's day in the 1840's.

> '*Ladies either undress in the sand or proceed in their bathing dresses at early dawn to the sea.... Some rush in recklessly as though it were a disagreeable process the sooner over the better, others timidly and by degrees approach the water, and so undergo their ablutions. Crowds of idlers parade the beach, and at every corner groups of sailors etc. lie all their length in the sun, and with hats over their eye luxuriate in a slumberous quiet. The only sign of activity to be met with in the streets, is the policeman buttoned up in his sweltering uniform, with oilskin hat, and stiff black smock, parading about in search of offenders, when the thermometer in the shade is almost at fever heat.*'

Not everyone behaved themselves which may have been a reason for the dawn bathing for '*the practice of looking over the sea-banks, immediately above the place where the ladies are bathing seems to be on the increase.*' The following year, 1849, a warning proclamation against trespass on the ladies' sands delivered by the Village Bellman was thought to have been a joke got up by '*waggish young ladies*' to give the Bellman a benefit. Soon after however there was a reminder that this '*unmanly practice*' was no laughing matter and that it was a punishable offence to cross the boundary line.

*　　*　　*　　*　　*　　*　　*

Around 1850 there was an attempt to stress the separateness of the South End from the rest of Spittal by styling it '*Newtown*'. This name, which can be seen on the 1852 map, never really caught on though and was only occasionally used. More defining was the spate of new building in the 1850's which much increased holiday accommodation.

Local papers then had a practice of printing the names of summer visitors along with their lodging house. A list of mid-July 1863 showed there then to have been thirty-one of these. That the 1822 Directory had included only four shows the growth of the summer trade. Brighton

House (nine rooms) boasted baths *'supplied by pipes direct from the sea'.* So too did Windsor Cottage, the water pumped by a windmill which was a striking feature of the Spittal skyline for several decades until blown down in a storm. Roxburgh House (nine rooms) and Roxburgh Place (fourteen rooms) offered an *'extensive and uninterrupted view of the German Ocean'* while Seafield House was *'well adapted for parties wishing to keep lodgers during the bathing season'.* As the last implies, owners sometimes let houses out for a tenant to conduct the summer operation. Occasionally a house reverted to private use as Roxburgh House did for a while.

The Press was happy to promote its virtues.

'To our lady readers we may confidently recommend the resort as the best bracer of nerves extant - whilst the genial breeze as a cosmetic for restoring colour to the cheeks and animation to the frame has in its beneficial results – no equal.'

Though it had a word of warning to bathers.

'A heated state is at all times to be avoided as dangerous and too much care cannot be taken that the body is perfectly cool before submitting it to the action of the water.'

The writer of these lines may have been mindful of the fate of Mr. John Wakenshaw of Etal who had a fit and died after sea-bathing. Undercurrents though were the biggest danger. In 1863 bathers were given the encouragement of six *'nice new bathing machines'.* From one of these on an August day two men emerged and found themselves in a powerful current. One managed to struggle ashore but the other, a compositor on *The Warder*, was swept out to sea and drowned. A young Duns draper had perished in the same way seven years earlier.

Disasters apart, proprietors were clearly taking pains to display their houses in the most attractive light, to be ready for the day in Sheldon's verse –

*'When fervid days of sultry heat set in
And drive the gentry here to splash and swim.'*

For in 1863 it was noted: *'We have never seen the village looking tidier, or their little flower pots prettier than this season....'* Sheldon had had his own recipe for popularity. *'It wants but some worn out debauchee or blasé nobleman to give the fashion to it, and then behold what changes.'* His wish was to be partly answered with the appearance on the scene of the arch-cad and noble bounder, Major Yelverton.

George Jackson noted Major Yelverton's presence on the beach. Anyone who had been reading the papers and recognised him would have glanced at him with more than casual curiosity. To say that he'd been getting a bad press would be putting it mildly. To the *Daily News* he was *'a lawless and ruthless social pirate'* with *'the morals of a monkey'*. The *Morning Post's* judgement was even more dire. *'Never before was human nature so bespattered with the mire of its own creation.'* Thus the Press in March 1861.

A few years before it had been very different. He'd returned from the Crimea in heroic style with a medal and clasp for his part in the actions at Inkerman and Sebastopol and been created a knight of the Fifth Class of Medjidie by the Turkish Government.

A chance meeting a few years before the Crimean War led to his plunge from fame to infamy. While aboard a Channel Ferry he'd met Maria Ann Longworth. The two hit it off and agreed to correspond. The daughter of a silk manufacturer, she quarrelled with her father over religious issues, the rift driving her abroad where she lived with her married sister in France or with friends in Austria. At the outbreak of the Crimean War she joined the French Sisters of Charity and was working for them at Galata Hospital when there was a chance meeting with Major Yelverton. He proposed to her and she accepted.

After the war there were a couple of curious weddings. In April 1857 Yelverton read aloud the marriage service in Miss Longworth's Edinburgh lodgings. They were later married by a priest in a Roman Catholic Chapel at Rostrevor in Ireland and lived together there and in Scotland. But in June 1858, while they were apart, he suddenly married the widow of Professor Forbes, for financial gain it was generally believed.

The Major justified this action on the grounds that his marriage to Maria Longworth had no legal validity in English law on account of the nature and location of the services. She maintained they'd been legally conducted and began a series of actions to prove it had been so which were to last for nine years.

Whatever legal merit the Major's position had it was hardly a gallant posture. By the time the case first came to court in Dublin in 1861 it was headline news. The Press pitted Maria Longworth against *'one of the meanest and most black-hearted scoundrels that disgrace the British Peerage,' 'a man who displayed beastly sensualism, the cool, calculating villainy of the practised seducer'*. When judgement was given in her favour cheering crowds in the packed streets bore her off to her lodgings in triumph.

The Dublin success was though to be followed by years of reverses. The Scottish Court of Session annulled the marriage and the House of Lords affirmed this decision in a majority judgement. Their Lordships were not through with the case though. When it returned they showed some irritation with Maria Longworth's vacillations and requests for adjournments and laid down strict ground rules for the giving of evidence. But neither here nor in a final appeal to the Court of Session in Edinburgh did she get any satisfaction.

Maria Longworth supported herself by writing, nearly all her earnings going into her litigation. In her later years she travelled widely, dying in South Africa. Major Yelverton, suspended by his regiment at the height of the affair, became the Fourth Viscount Avonmore. If he had married a second time for money then he was disappointed for he got very little. The affair became the stuff of novels with such titles as *A Wife and not a Wife*.

*　　*　　*　　*　　*　　*　　*

As George Jackson observed, the natives and the summer visitors inhabited different worlds and had little in common. Yet one Spittaler, who'd managed to annul his Lamberton marriage, must have felt something of a bond with the Major.

4 The 1836 whaling voyage of the *Norfolk*

As the *Norfolk* pulled clear of Berwick Harbour in the Spring of 1836 its crew must have been hoping for better fortune. Trapped in Arctic pack-ice the previous September it had been unable to make it back to its home port until January, the crew weak but all surviving.This voyage though was to be far worse as the diary entries of Thomas Crowther show.

From 1807 the *Norfolk* (309 tons) and the New York-built *Lively* (209 tons) operated out of Berwick as whalers. They were the largest vessels on the Berwick Register. The *Norfolk* was acquired when its Tyneside owner went bankrupt. It was described as *'square-rigged with a sturdy bowsprit, square sterned, carvel built but with no galleries and no figurehead'*. For the first few years of their joint operation *Lively* was more successful but thereafter *Norfolk* pulled ahead. Lively was though also employed in the herring and timber trade.

Whalers generally left port in February or March with the aim of being on Arctic station by Mid-May. By the time it was ready for sea the *Norfolk* had mustered thirty-one men, well short of its complement of fifty. This was not unusual as it was standard practice to sign on additional crew at Stromness where too provisions could be topped up.

Captain Harrison headed the crew list. An experienced whaler, he had been master of the *Norfolk* sinse 1827. The two mates, surgeon, and bosun came from Edinburgh or East Lothian while the crew was local: from Berwick, Tweedmouth,Spittal, Ancroft, and East Ord. Eight of the crew were listed as Spittalers, three boatsteerers, two line managers, and three apprentices. In addition there were Thomas Crowther and Thomas Hall. both listed under 'Tweedmouth'. The first was to have a long connection with Spittal while the second, in his twenty-fourth season as a harpooner aboard the *Norfolk*, was to be described by Captain Harrison as a Spittaler.

The *Norfolk* picked up an additional nineteen crew at Stromness and then headed for the perils of the Arctic. A degree of confidence could come from being aboard a robustly durable vessel like *Truelove* of Hull *('as handy as a cutter,as safe as a lifeboat')* which made seventy-two trips. The *Norfolk*, about to embark on its thirtieth season, also had a reputation for knowing its way round Arctic wastes. But a ship returning intact did not mean that its crew would.

The various trades to be found aboard had different levels of risk. Chanciest was that of harpooner operating from a six-oared, whale-chasing boat. Coopering or sailmaking, though vital, lacked such drama. But there were hazards all faced. Chief among these was that of the ship being crushed and the crew marooned on the ice with the probability of severe frostbite if they survived. There was the danger of fire from carrying such an inflammable cargo as blubber: this was demonstrated in 1823 when *Fame* of Hull was totally destroyed in Stromness harbour. Then there were the Spring gales of the North Atlantic to contend with. In 1822 the *Norfolk* lost its master, Captain Stephens, and three seamen who were all swept overboard. Finally, there was the by now preventable disease of scurvy which continued to take its toll.

*   *   *   *   *   *   *

Whaling had been a steadily expanding trade since about 1760. By the early 1830's there were over a hundred and fifty British whalers. In some areas it had become a key employer. In 1825 there were 1400 Shetlanders aboard 70 whalers, despite the opposition of the lairds to the trade. A sense of the scale of the trade is given by the 3,528 whales killed in 1832/33 and the 360 casks on board the *Norfolk* at the time of its sale. A feature of whaling was its fluctuating fortune. This can be seen in the catches made by *Norfolk* and *Lively*.

Years	No.of Trips	Total Catch	Most Whales	Least Whales	App. Ave.
1807-1812	12	155	25	4	13
1814-1819	12	73	16	2	6
1820-1829	16	125	19	2	8

Differing catches meant that the volume of whale oil produced varied markedly too: for instance, 308 tons in 1808 and a mere 54 in 1811. Whale oil volumes measured profit or loss. The largest single source of demand was for lighting.This accounted for nearly half the total output until gas lighting began to replace it around 1820. It was used too in at least a dozen other industrial processes including the allied trades of sail-making, rope-making, and shipbuilding.

Anyone investing in whaling needed capital to ride out the lean years and a robust confidence in the earning potential of the business. Such a man was the Newcastle entrepreneur, Thomas Richard Batson, co-owner of the *Lively* until it was wrecked in The Davis Straits, a substantial investor in the *Norfolk*, and a Director of the Tweed Bank.

His optimism must have seemed fully justified by the end of the 1834 season. The *Norfolk* had enjoyed unprecedented success, catching eighty-four whales in three years.

There were plenty of barrels to float down the Tweed on the ebb tide to the Spittal strand. From here they were taken to the Greenland Yard on the Point where the blubber was placed in huge furnaces and prodded at intervals by men with long poles. The blubber was boiled for three or four hours in a process speedy but dreadfully smelly. Aromatically, Sandstell Road was not the best place to live, the whale factory being followed by the equally whiffy manure factories. Coastguards and Excise kept a close watch on production to tally the tax payable on each barrel of whale oil.

*   *   *   *   *   *   *

In keeping with the character of the trade the years following the boom of the early 1830's were poor. 1835 produced only a single whale and by early August of 1836 Captain Harrison had made just two killings. This and the sighting of whales in Melville Bay may have induced him to remain longer. Lingering in order to try to augment a modest catch was the prime cause of whalers getting iced up.

As he wrote to the owners: *'I remained in South East Bay, that place from which I last wrote you; as long as there were any fish to be seen....'* Following whale sightings, *'On the 7th August I entered Melville Bay and on the 10th got into the west water but found the prospect so bad that I immediately returned to look for a passage out.'* But it was too late. *'We were frozen up in Melville Bay and after I got liberated I made my way into the west water.'*

The *Norfolk* had been released from the ice after twenty-four hours and from then on she was searching for a way through the ice. But on October 8th she was stuck fast again and this time it was to be more than five months before she was freed. At least she had company. The *Grenville Bay* and the *Dee* were also frozen up and these vessels were never more than a mile apart. Five or six miles to the north-east were the equally immobile *Swan* and *Advice*. The *Thomas* had been wrecked and some of her crew taken aboard the *Norfolk*.

Being stuck in the ice meant enduring the depressing effect of cold and dark, physical deterioration or at best acute discomfort, and a dull foreboding at times turning to terror when the grinding of the ice threatened the ship.Thomas Crowther had already been held in the ice for three months when the surviving portion of his diary commences:

'Jan.16th. One man died on board the Dee *and a great many are lying badly on board of her. We saw the sun today for the first time after the absence of 61 days. All men were called on deck to see if they could go on less provisions as our beef is running short. Three pieces of beef are boiled each day to serve 45 men.'*

Then, seemingly, what they most dreaded.

'At 7 p.m. the ice closed very rapidly towards our ship,pieces from four to six feet thick turning one over the other from three to four tons in weight, which put us all in great alarm. We got our provisions on to the ice and put our sick men into a boat which we covered over with canvas to keep them from the cold winds and snow as some of them were unable to walk, and it was impossible to get them to any of the other ships.'

But the threat passed.

'Thank God we have been highly favoured for when the ice was pressing close on us it suddenly stopped and came no further. Every man who was able had his clothes and chest in readiness to go on the ice. Thank God we had moonlight at the time.'

A vessel held fast in the ice was not stationary. Ice drift could carry it some three hundred miles a month. The stresses imposed by this movement were a continual threat.

'The ice has been opening and closing around us all night. We got an observation from the sun and found our-selves in Lat. 69 degrees N. Another man died on the Dee *and there is not sufficient food to support the others who are sick.'*

Below deck the temperature hovered around -6 degrees F. even with a lit stove. On January 18th there was a flicker of hope with the opening up of a stretch of water leading to the open sea but it had iced up two hours later. Three days later Crowther was writing:

'Jan.21. The four ships are all in sight today. Our coal is getting scarce. A fox was seen alongside our ship today but before the gun was got ready he escaped. These animals travel a long way from land. We are all becoming very weak owing to our poor diet. Most of our men have sore mouths and are all stuck out with

spots on the legs. Five of them are in bed.'

In fact they had more than enough salt beef. As Captain Harrison was to write later:

'I was not distressed for lack of provisions but the men could not eat the salt beef and hard bread, the scurvy being so bad in their mouths.'

Things were though even worse on the *Dee* as Crowther recorded:

'No water or land to be seen. The ship is drifting south at the rate of about two miles in 24 hours. The ice is still very still. Men are dying daily on the Dee. *It is very disheartening to see them dropping off and all of us so weak.'*

Captain Harrison was badly affected by the death of the *Dee's* captain. Crowther again:

Feb 4 A signal from the Dee *to say that the captain had died in the night. His body has been placed in a coffin to be taken home if it is the Lord's will to liberate us.*

An attempt at relief was though under way. In January a bounty had been offered for discovery of the missing whalers. The *Lord Gambier* and the *Lady Jane* set out on the search.

On March 29th the ice finally yielded and the *Norfolk* was able to reach open water. She had the great good fortune to meet with the *Lord Gambier* the following day and to be the first of the missing ships to be reprovisioned. something that probably saved a number of lives. As James Johnson wrote in a letter to his wife:

I have to thank God that I have the opportunity of writing to you again: but if we had not fallen in with supplies from the Lord Gambier *we should have been all down. All we had to conduct the ship was fourteen in number, but we came very fast about after receiving fresh food, with the help of God."*

The *Norfolk* headed for Stromness, a port used to the sight of battered whalers limping over the horizon. The previous year the *Viewforth* had returned after being trapped in the ice with only seven of its eighty-four strong crew fit for duty and a number of amputations needed. A letter from Stromness described the return of three of the whalers in chilling terms:

The Whaling Vessel, The *Lord Gambier*, in Kirkcaldy Harbour, 1860

Captain Warham wrote the following to the ship's owner at the mouth of the Davis Straits on March 31 1837. *'About sunset last night a strange sail hove into sight to which we bore down in a fresh breeze from the northward, and in a short time I had the pleasure of going aboard the* Norfolk. *..... Many of the people are sick, and out of sixty hands, including a number from the crew of the ship* Thomas, *sixteen have already died.'* After nearly thirty years operating as a whaler from the Tyne she was re-registered at Kirkcaldy in 1853 but was lost in the Davis Straits in 1862 soon after this early photograph was taken.

© Fife County Museums: Kirkcaldy Museum and Art Gallery

*Three of the ice-bound whalers came in here yesterday, viz.
The* Norfolk, Dee, *and* Grenville Bay..... *Such a scene I never
witnessed; dead men lying about the decks, their companions
scarcely able to throw them overboard. The* Dee *of Aberdeen had
only one man that could go aloft when she came into harbour.'*

Losses had been heavy. Of the 250 men aboard the five vessels 140 had
perished. Captain Harrison reported that the *Dee* had lost 44 men and
the Grenville Bay 20. The *Norfolk's* losses were lighter. There were three
Orcadians and five Englishmen, among them the harpooner Thomas
Hall and the sailmaker George Leith. The other eight deaths recorded by
Captain Harrison must have been from the rescued Thomas' crew. There
was little return for the suffering. *'I am sorry to say I have but two whales,'*
the captain informed the owners. In the first few days of May the *Norfolk*
inched ever closer to its home port. Then, on May 4th, as The *Berwick
Advertiser* reported:

*The news that she was in sight flew like lightning from mouth to
mouth; and the ramparts speedily became a scene of great bustle,
being crowded with a number of delighted gazers. At 6 o'clock
Captain Harrison, the surgeon and some of the crew landed at
the pier which was covered with people - all anxious to greet the
adventurers with a hearty welcome.'*

The Mayor and two of the owners were among the welcoming party.
Captain Harrison reckoned that the rest of the crew *'were but poorly'* and
all but two of them were able to walk off the vessel.

*　　*　　*　　*　　*　　*　　*

One salutary effect of the deaths from scurvy was legislation compelling
whalers to carry lime juice or other anti-scorbutics. The lack of this can
only have been gross negligence or misguided economy. After all, many
decades earlier Captain Cook had grasped the cause of scurvy and made
every effort to prevent it. Parliament was only able to act with such speed
as the remedy was generally known.

The *Norfolk* made one final voyage the following year but made only
one killing and was sold in 1838 by its now nine owners. Its principal
investor, Thomas Richard Batson, went bankrupt.

Whaling began to decline. Seemingly whale stocks never recovered
from the slaughter of the early 1830's. The invention of the Svend Feyn

harpoon gun in the 1880's further imperilled survival. Reduced numbers also meant that whaling became less profitable and more hazardous. By The First World War whalers were only occasionally to be seen in port.

A reminder that not all was passivity during those long, dark days in the ice can be seen in the detailed, intricate whalebone carvings in Stromness Museum. A local memento are the crossed harpoons on the door of No. 1, Wellington Terrace.

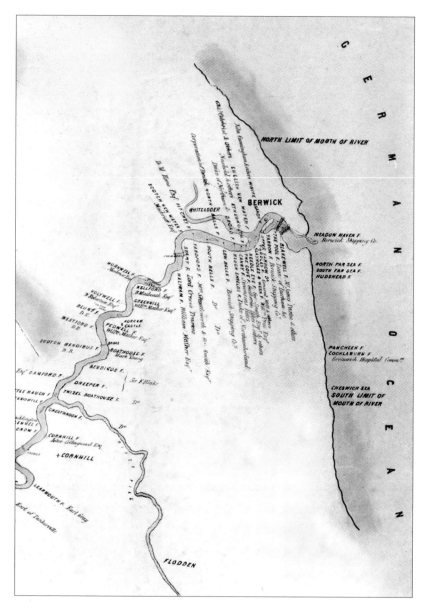

Proprietors and Netting Stations on the Lower Tweed, circa 1860

Drawn by Thomas Mitchell of Melrose, Engineer and Surveyor

5 Salmon fishing: Tweed Acts and Tweed Wars

There was a generally buoyant mood in the local economy during the 1850's. Charles Wilson of Hawick, speaking at the Mayor's dinner of 1853, reckoned the previous year *'one of continuous prosperity'*.

Salmon fishermen saw encouraging prospects ahead. The decade had started badly, 1851 being *'the most unproductive season we have any record of.'* There had too been problems with dyes flowing into the Tweed from the Chirnside works. Recent railway work had though made distant markets more accessible and the future seemed set fair.

In 1856 though a cloud appeared on the horizon with the news that the Upper Tweed Proprietors were introducing to Parliament a Tweed Bill. This, it was naturally assumed, would introduce measures favouring the angler at the expense of the licensed net fisherman.When more was learnt of its provisions some alarm was felt and the Lower Proprietors tried to run a counter-Bill against it.

Yet there was a general belief that any Bill that the Upper Proprietors did succeed in getting through Parliament would prove no more than mildly vexatious. The composition of the Commons Committee seemed encouraging. Given the atmosphere of this free-trading, anti-regulatory era it seemed inconceivable that the demands of anglers should be favoured above those of industry and the Tweed allowed to become *'a mere sporting river'*.

What emerged from Parliament in August 1857 was a shock. That the measures the Act embodied should be almost uniformly to the advantage of the Upper Proprietors was no great surprise but their drastic scope was. In particular, clauses dealing with the length of the close season and the use of nets seemed to impose crippling restrictions. The intrusiveness which it legitimised, in the form of house searches, caused bitter resentment in the wider community and led to a riot in Spittal in October1859 , and to much subsequent unrest. By this time bailiffs were reluctant to visit Spittal without police protection.

The Tweed Commissioners, a body dominated by the Upper Proprietors, were not yet satisfied though and in the further Acts of 1859, 1861, and 1863 they tightened their grip, determined to have the mastery of the rod enshrined in law. They seemed close to demanding total control of all activity on the river. One commissioner was heard to query the legality of the steam ferry that plied between Spittal and Berwick as it might obstruct the free run of the fish and thus be deemed to be committing an offence. Other interests counted for little with them and with the strength of the County vote solidly behind the Acts there seemed little hope of redress.

*   *   *   *   *   *   *

The Close Season had originally been a six-week spell enforced by the Corporation. Since then successive Acts had stipulated increasingly lengthy periods until the 1857 Act required a six-month lay-off. Though the House of Lords knocked fourteen days off, the effect of this enforced inactivity was bound to be severe. The Corporation considered petitioning Parliament as its own fishing interest was involved but was advised by Berwick's M.P.'s, Messrs. Marjoribanks and Stapleton, that any such protest would have little effect. To add to the sense of injustice the Close Season for rod angling, which had been briefer, was reduced to a mere two months in the 1859 Act. Later it was claimed that the fungoid disease,which became a serious problem, was the result of overcrowding in the river.

The use of nets was tightly regulated. When the legal basis of a charge had been obstructing the free run of the fish the use made of a net as well as its design had to be considered. There were grey areas. In 1853 James Smith was taken to court and fined although he'd been using the same sole and near-wall nets for twenty-three years. Three years later, the Berwick Shipping Company, which had extensive salmon fishing interests, was forced to withdraw its fixed nets.

Much of the evidence taken by the House of Commons before the 1857 Act concerned the use of nets. Reports that the sole and stell nets might be banned reached the Lower Proprietors. Alexander Mitchell, Superintendent of the Tweed Commissioners saw no fault with the upward stell net as long as it was properly used but others were urging a ban on this and other nets. Those who wanted greater restriction carried the day. All fixed nets were to be banned as was *'any net held by hand or otherwise for any period of time'.* Stake, bag, bob, hang,sole, stell and cairn nets were all declared illegal.

The Commissioners went further. The mere possession of one of these nets was made an offence. Bailiffs were given the authority of police constables and empowered to enter ground bordering the river and to search houses - though for this they had to have grounds of suspicion and a search warrant. The execution of this part of the Act would have exercised the most tactful authority. With the bailiffs the situation quickly became inflammatory.

A further ground of contention was the operation of the Tweed Acts beyond the river mouth. This was not new but the area under restriction had grown. The 1859 Act banned salmon fishing seven miles north and south of the pier and five miles out to sea. While the right of riparian proprietors to control the fishing in their waters was generally acknowledged the exercise of these same powers in the ocean was often disputed. Why should Spittal fishermen be put in a worse position than those of Dunbar or The Tyne – worse too than foreign vessels bound only by the three-mile limit?

*   *   *   *   *   *   *

For the Acts to prove effective a substantial bailiff force was going to be needed. The complex provisions of the Acts meant that the licensed trade was going to need closer supervision. But poaching was rather more in the minds of the Tweed Commissioners, especially in view of the six-month Close Season.

Previous Tweed Acts had been enforced with patchy success. The Upper River had been particularly problematic. John Grey, writing in 1843, reckoned that the extent of the brazen day-time fishing had rendered the Tweed Acts virtually a dead letter and that all they were doing was fostering a disregard for the law.

Stiff financial penalties, with gaol for those unable to pay, were relied on as a deterrent. When, in January 1844, Francis and Thomas Elliott were caught with forty-four bull trout the tariff was *'not less than a pound and not more than ten pounds for each and every offence'*. Unable to find forty-four pounds the pair paid their second visit to Durham Gaol. Later, in the summer of that year, when another pair of Spittalers, George and Joshua Johnson were caught illegally using a T net in the Tweed they discovered that the minimum penalty had been increased to ten pounds. Some of the brawling with bailiffs may well have been intimidatory, an attempt to stop them giving the evidence that could well mean gaol.

By the early 1850's the Tweed Commissioners felt they were getting the upper hand. *'The Police Commissioner has a confident opinion that at no period has poaching been so nearly abolished,'* was reported in 1852. The need for increased vigilance in the wake of the Tweed Acts was though shown with the appointment of twenty-four bailiffs to protect the lower river. The Upper Proprietors presciently warned of the danger of future conflict. They can hardly though have anticipated anything on the scale of what did shortly take place.

The *Berwick Advertiser* reported the following events on a mid-October Monday of 1859.

> *'There was a rather serious riot at Spittal, at the mouth of the Tweed, on Monday night. The day had been stormy, which had the double effect of bringing large quantities of salmon from the sea into the river, and of preventing the prosecution of the white fishing. So, pretty well the whole of the village turned out, not merely to a man, but to a woman, to engage in salmon poaching. Eight boats were manned, and were supported by the populace on shore, all armed with slings. They not only drove thirteen water bailiffs over to the Berwick side, but gave chase, captured the bailiffs' boat, and sunk her. The men were disguised in their wives' bedgowns, and there is likely to be some difficulty in identification.'*

The following night, rejoicing in victory, a number of Spittalers put out in five cobles, trawling the mouth of the Tweed for salmon. The Town Council, alarmed, issued a proclamation warning others from joining or supporting the rioters. A week later, with the rioters' disguises still not penetrated, there was a different incident.

During the afternoon Mr. Fletcher's fishmonger's cart was brought to a halt at Sunnyside by a group of six bailiffs, one of them grabbing the horse's bridle. Annoyed at being thus peremptorily stopped Mr. Fletcher leapt from his cart with his whip and laid about him to some effect. *'Down they go. One. Two. Three !'* Then a blow stunned Mr. Fletcher and some bailiffs knelt on top of him. Six bailiffs being deemed an insufficient force to take him in charge reinforcements were sent for. Taking advantage of this hiatus Mr.Fletcher's boy whipped the horse into action and it galloped off towards Berwick, a few bailiffs hanging on for a while but soon forced to let go.

The bailiffs had been on the prowl after picking up rumours of illegally landed fish. These could have been deliberately spread. A handy diversionary tactic was to persuade the bailiffs of some supposed wrongdoing, then have them hare off on a wild-goose chase leaving the river mouth unpatrolled. The station was a favourite lure, searches there generally taking a while. Foul fish were though sometimes found on trains, some addressed to non-existent firms such as 'Pollard Bros.' and later there were to be searches inside Billingsgate itself.

The search for the illicit fish brought two bailiffs that same evening to the Spittal premises of Mr. Mathison, a cooper. After drawing a blank with the barrels and tubs in his yard they wanted to look round his house but first had to send to Berwick for a search warrant. Mr. Mathison civilly invited them inside for some coffee but they, seeming to suspect some ruse, opted to remain outside. *'I suppose it's fish you want, not coffee, but you will have to wait a long time,'* he remarked. While waiting for the warrant the bailiffs started quarrelling, one got drunk, and in the presence of a gathering crowd had to be taken away by the police. No fish were found.

That eventful October concluded with another major engagement in which a force of thirteen bailiffs and four policemen, searching for nets in Spittal, found itself confronted by a huge, stone-throwing crowd.

> *'They made an onslaught upon the suspected delinquents, seized several nets etc., and made off with their prize. They had not proceeded far, however, when they were set upon by the 'natives', male and female; and, after a brief but determined engagement, the officers were beat off, and were compelled to relinquish their recently captured booty.'*

In the dusky confusion there was a severe struggle between two men who each thought the other a bailiff.

Unrest continued the following year, the house searches causing bitter resentment and the fishermen retaliating by stoning the steamer. Mrs Lough suffered the indignity of having her bed examined, the bailiffs finding it highly amusing, she giving them a piece of her mind. Complaints of ransacked houses came too from The Greenses.

Some argued for a stronger police presence. Others demurred. Why should policemen *'do the dirty work of water bailiffs'*? No doubt there were other reasons for not wanting an excess of policemen around but a public meeting called to consider the use of the County Police rejected the idea. The Town Council, which tended to take a cavalier attitude to such resolutions found that it was not consulted. The Watch Committee, with its brief for police matters, held itself solely responsible. It voted by four votes to three to introduce the County Police, the four in favour, the Mayor, and Councillors Gilchrist, Clay, and Ramsey all having salmon fishing interests, the other three not. The decision, and the way it was reached, sparked protest. *'Was it decorous? Was it legal?'* asked *The Berwick Journal.*

The Town Council could permit major undertakings to drift along for decades withour effective resolution but groups of Councillors sometimes moved nimbly in the protection or furtherance of their interests. Cllr. Ramsey had earlier sparked controversy by voting for himself as Mayor – a decisive vote as it happened.

*　　*　　*　　*　　*　　*　　*

When Major Browne and the County Police appeared on the scene a sharp contrast was noted between their general propriety and the *'ruffianly violence'* often used by the bailiffs. The Tweed Acts had given bailiffs the powers of constables but they had yet to acquire their disciplines. Major Browne soon found cause for complaint and had one discharged and two reprimanded.

The low opinion of the bailiffs was reflected in the local Press. While the main problem was undoubtedly the *'radically and irredeemably bad law'* its enforcement with *'harsh and irritating severity'* by *'men of such rotten reputation that one cannot but regard them with ineffable disgust'* made matters a good deal worse.

A recruitment source was suggested.

> For *'if the respectable gentlemen who are now in their employ, and whose province it appears to be to search women and smash in the skulls of innocent men, are insufficient for the purpose, then let them advertise for a dozen returned convicts or superannuated pugilists.'*

Their numbers too aroused comment. It seemed that *'the body of officers prowling about the banks to detect illegal fishing is something absurdly numerous'*. Altogether too much was being seen of *'the officious band of bailiffs'*. Did they get the fish? Did that explain their zeal?

Maybe the headstrong methods of some blackened the name of all. And of course any job which involves regular stoning and where the threat of violence lurks in the background is bound to be testing. Many poachers when caught did not go quietly. William McAdam *'offered great violence'*. The stones sometimes found their mark. The bailiff Robert English suffered a serious head wound when one penetrated the steamer's netting. Nor some nights was it easy to see what was taking place round The Carr Rock, the lamp being regularly extinguished. Cllr. Ramsey was sure the poachers were doing this.

The Tweed Commissioners considered the Borough Police Force was not pulling its weight. In October 1861, at a time when the bailiffs were unable to enter Spittal without police protection, they sent a Memorial to the Secretary of State complaining of the inefficiency of the force. Yet there was clearly a limit to what a four-man body could do. A few years earlier Superintendent Anderson had asked the Town Council for more men but received a dusty, rather rude response.

The most violent assault in this phase of the long agitation over the Tweed Acts occurred in September 1863. Water Bailiff Maclean around midnight spotted '*bobbing*' on the river and on going to investigate thought he could identify Robert Carr, George Elliott, and Prideaux Patterson, all White Fishermen with no business there. In the subsequent fracas he was kicked until insensible, later managing to crawl to a water trough where he fainted. Passing out three more times on his way, it took him three hours to reach his home. Dr. McLagan considered his head wounds had been caused by extreme violence and he was off duty for two months.

When the case came up at the Northumberland Assizes the following March the jury promptly acquitted Carr and Elliott, the alibi evidence counting strongly in their favour. Prideaux Patterson though had gone on the run. A man frequently before the magistrates for assaults, mainly Saturday night set-to's but capable of starting a rumpus over almost anything – one was over a bird's nest – he must have realised that this was a case of a different order. Five pounds was offered for his apprehension. An additional suspect, Ralph Havery, who had reportedly been seen striking Maclean over the head with a soda water bottle, was brought forward for trial.

This fearsome attack seems to have had a sobering effect for the next few years were comparatively uneventful.

*　　*　　*　　*　　*　　*　　*

The Upper Proprietors weren't yet satisfied though. In March 1861 they had another Bill, a '*crushing and despotic measure*' under way in the Commons. Its aim was to bring back the start of the Close Season three weeks to August 24th. Then an 1863 Act extended the operation of the Tweed Acts into Berwickshire. At the same time, they were widely suspected of using the Boards of Management which they'd got formed and dominated to devise ways of evading the increased ratings which their actions had made necessary.

The commercial outlook seemed gloomy.

'The Legislature having made a present of the waters for a place

of amusement for the aristocracy we apprehend ... the commercial doings of the river will cease to be of any value.'

It wanted only the arrival of the expected gunboat, and with it the crushing of the poachers, to make their victory complete. In 1889, during another period of unrest over the Tweed Acts, the objectors, now strongly supported by the Town Council, many of whose members had manufacturing interests and who were fed up with the fuss and cost of Tweed protection, it was noted that while the rental value of the angling waters had risen steadily since the middle of the century that of the netting stations had remained fairly static. Indeed, by this date some former stations had been abandoned. Many blamed the 1857/1859 Tweed Acts for the lack of growth in the netting industry.

6 Herring fishing

With the approach of the herring fishing season many hopefuls trudged towards the ports where they might subsequently be seen whittling a stick, the recognised sign of a man seeking work.

Getting engaged could be profitable, the chance to make some eight pounds in a short season not to be lightly passed up. The scale of the trade was prodigious. In two August mornings at Whitby in 1862 some eight million herring were landed, realising some three thousand pounds. Spittal was not in this league but the volume was still considerable, its thirty-odd boats were averaging 170 crans during an August week of 1848. Assuming, as the writer Charles Weld did, that there were 750 herring to the cran, some 382,500 fish would have been landed. A more homely figure was the price of three for a penny in Berwick market.

The trade had been artificially boosted by the Government with the offer of bounties to restrict Dutch influence in the North Sea. While these were restricted to decked vessels of sixty tons or more they were of little relevance to Spittal. In 1797 though the barrel became the basis of the bounty: two shillings per barrel with an additional two shillings and eightpence for each one exported. In 1815 four shillings a barrel was offered. Here was a real incentive to pursue the trade.

* * * * * * *

Herring fishing was a gamble and perhaps that was part of its attraction. In one season a boat might make a hefty profit, in another struggle even to cover expenses. Boats fishing at no great distance from each other could return with markedly different catches, some with a heavy load, others almost clean.

One ingredient of a successful season was the avoidance of hazards. The fish themselves could produce a dire effect. A shoal could fill the nets with an unsustainable weight that meant the loss of nets and fish. Storms and wrecks could also take their toll of nets while a sharp lookout had to be kept for steamers.

Then there were the French. By the early Victorian period French vessels were far more numerous than Dutch. In the guise of buyers they were welcomed and sought out. But they came too as competitors with acknowledged skill in locating shoals, put down to the periods their vessels spent continuously at sea. Their inshore fishing caused complaint, in particular their habit of shooting their nets across the local, lighter ones which could *'tear all our men's nets to pieces'*. One boat lost sixteen nets in August 1859. Other owners generally helped a boat that had suffered serious loss for speedy replacement was necessary if idle days in a short season were to be avoided.

There were occasional tries for herring out of season such as the odd Spring trip to the Firth of Forth but the season proper usually ran from mid-July till early September. Taken earlier the fish were immature, lacking plumpness. The appearance of whales and dogfish was taken as a sign that there were shoals around, dogfish unwelcome as they ate the herring in the nets.

Others besides regular fishermen looked to take their chance with the herring. One such was William Robertson, a Berwick Hill miner who owned fifty pounds worth of fishing gear. He was allowed to go off fishing if enough coal had been worked. In 1865 it hadn't but he went anyway. Taken to court, his argument that he'd been going to the fishing for the last seventeen years was found inadequate. Fined ten shillings, he was not the first miner to be told the difference between custom and law by the magistrates. Two similar cases followed.

*   *   *   *   *   *   *

The statement in the 1806 directory that *'Mr. Strangeways lately built a herring house here after the same plan as those in Tweedmouth'* suggests that this was the first such. By 1822 there were seven functioning yards, a number that altered little in the next thirty years. Among them were the Master Herring Curers John Alexander who worked in the trade for over forty years and Alexander Alexander, owner of an alarming dog and a rather too tempting garden. The Berwick trader George Bogue had a yard and also established a ropery while James Cowe took over the Whale Oil factory site after the sale of the *Norfolk*.

By the middle of the century the trade had become a key part of Spittal's economy as Sheldon noted. *'Herring houses abound in Spittal and the herring boats drawn up on the beach by their number attest the importance of the fish as an article of value.'* In 1848 the Greenses' forty-five boats and Spittal's thirty were together occupying three hundred and seventy-five fishermen.

The curers though with their in-house coopering were the masters of the trade. A crew was deemed engaged to the curer once the number of crans to be supplied and the price had been agreed. Often there was another tie, the curer buying the boat and the owner paying for it in instalments. Spirits could feature in the terms of engagement, a practice roundly condemned by Captain Washington in his report on East Coast harbours. He argued too for a system of mutual insurance to replace the existing bounty payments. The coming of the railway introduced the 'fresh buyer' with ready money who often offered a higher price. But a season's contract offered more stability and financial obligations often left an owner with little real choice.

*   *   THE 1853 SEASON   *   *

Some years were memorable. A run of three good years culminated with a September day in 1837 when it was supposed *'there were more fish in Spittal that day than in the memory of man'.* Other particularly productive seasons were 1842, 1848, and 1850. 1853 too was a highly successful season despite the French threat.

The War Steamer, *Tartarus,* had previously patrolled the fishing grounds but her absence for much of the 1853 season, co-inciding with the refitting of the revenue cutter, *Eagle,* left a vacuum which the French readily filled. The three mile limit was widely ignored with as many as eighty of the *'lumbering French trawlers'* found within the bounds, the boldest *'approaching to the very harbour mouths'.* One Spittal boat had thirteen nets swept out of the water. Twenty-two enraged skippers went to the customs house to complain of the unlawful damage only to find that the officers had gone home. Elsewhere it was a similar story. Some fifty French boats were fishing off North Sunderland with the local crews mostly scared away, *'beat off from fishing'* by their aggression. To add insult to injury a French Government vessel was hovering in the background but refused to do more than check that its fishermen were complying with French tax law by claiming a bounty only for fish caught and not for any bought.

A naval presence was needed and its absence resented. Why was the Government not more actively enforcing its legislation? Belatedly the *Tartarus* arrived from Leith and with *H.M.S. Archer* also on the scene the picture changed. Seeing *Tartarus* approach Captain Baptiste Zin of *St. Jean B 14* slipped the one hundred and forty nets he had set and pulled away leaving a small boat on station. The crew of this boat were warned that unless they signalled the *St. Jean* and persuaded her to return all the nets would be confiscated. The *St. Jean* returned and the captain was duly charged and fined. There was then a steady procession of other

French skippers through the Magistrates Court. Defences that drift or ignorance of the law accounted for their position were not accepted and heavy fines were levied.

Unusually the season lasted for over nine weeks at the end of which each boat was thought to have made an average profit of one hundred and ten pounds. The curers flourished, filling six thousand barrels at an agreed price the same or marginally higher than that offered five years before. This was despite the growing use of boxes, kits, and hampers to pack and despatch the fish. There was wide use of *'boxes of rude construction'* which would contain some hundred herrings in a bloater state and sell for six or seven shillings. The curers still had the upper hand.

By 1853 the herring fleet had become something of a spectacle, *'a mass of shipping, individually of tiny dimensions'*, Spittal's now forty-odd vessels being a part of a contingent of some three hundred (estimated at four hundred the following year). The trade was now thought to be employing about a thousand men, women, and children throughout the Borough.

*　　*　　*　　*　　*　　*　　*

In 1857 Dunbar merchants expressed displeasure at the leisurely pace of the Borough's fishermen. Dunbar crews had their fish ready for landing as their boats entered harbour. Berwick's tended to wander off for breakfast before attending to the fish. A more competitive spirit was urged. The curers though were also looking further afield, the growing export trade that year showing a fourfold increase in despatches to the Baltic.

The future was though looking rather uncertain. Whereas one Government measure, the introduction of the bounty, had greatly boosted the trade another, the proposed abolition of the Board of Fisheries, looked like damaging it. Government bodies seldom attract strong support but throughout 1856 there had been considerable agitation in favour of this one . Set up in 1809 it had seen the herring trade increase from 90,000 barrels then to 705,000 in 1855. One of its acts had been the introduction of the brand and a system of regular inspection as a quality guarantee. If the Board went so would the brand. That was almost certain to affect the curer's premium price.

Opponents of the Board didn't question its effectiveness but saw its regulatory powers as something of an anomaly in an age of Free Trade. Herring were a prime example. Why should herring be afforded such a degree of protectiveness when other fish by comparison were subject only to the play of market forces? The Board's defenders argued that it would be rash to dispense with a system which gave a proven guarantee of quality.

The strength of feeling prompted the appointment of three Government Commissioners to report on the brand. Lengthy lists of arguments were deployed for and against its retention, the one being largely the reverse of the other, with Free Trade v Protection providing the context. The Commissioners decided by two votes to one to preserve the brand and, in the event, both it and The Board of Fisheries survived.

An incident of 1858 showed the reputation and reach of the brand. A barrel found to contain rotten fish was landed at Harburg, displaying the initials 'D.C.'. These were supposedly those of an Eyemouth Inspector who was later shown to be a fiction.

At the start of the 1860's a new threat appeared in the form of the trawler from the south. It was claimed that these ravaged the spawning grounds, preventing fish from reaching maturity, and a petition to Parliament was got up.

By the 1870's trawlers were badly affecting the livelihood of the inshore fisherman.

7 The first two lifeboats

Everyone knew that shipping was a hazardous business. The collation and publication of details though brought home to the public the prodigious scale of the loss. In 1852, 1,115 vessels were wrecked with the loss of 900 lives. In the month of January 1856 alone there were 265 wrecks. The dispersal of this grim knowledge induced greater support for lifesaving bodies. The wreck of prestigious vessels like the *Royal Charter* made a deep impression as did the foundering of ships near land within sight of powerless spectators. The sinking of the *Christina* prompted activity in Berwick.

The *Christina* had sailed from Stockholm with a cargo of bones, tar, and deals. She approached the harbour with torn sails in a *'very boisterous sea with a high north-easterly wind'*. No pilot could reach her and she was directed by signals from the lighthouse watched by the crowd of spectators that had gathered on the pier. While crossing the bar she was struck by a heavy sea which flung her on her beam ends after which she was doomed. She floated for about ten minutes within a quarter of a mile of the pier then sank drowning all eight on board. Their bodies were later washed ashore.

*   *   *   *   *   *   *

The Royal Society for the Preservation of Life from Shipwreck had been founded in 1824 and was at first enthusiastically supported. In its first year it raised almost ten thousand pounds but this had dwindled to a mere two hundred and fifty-four pounds in its fifth year. In 1835, the year after the *Christina's* sinking, this body was approached with a view to stationing a boat at Berwick. It was though unable to grant the necessary two hundred pounds and a local subscription was decided on. This funded a thirty-foot, ten-oared boat.

It was first put to the test in 1837 by the *Margaret* of Dundee, a vessel of 120 tons, bound from Shields for Dundee with coals. A severe storm one Saturday night caused such serious leaking that her captain decided to run her aground on Spittal beach the next morning.

She beached opposite Brighton House and the crew took to the rigging. An attempt to shoot a line with Dunnett's rocket apparatus failed as did two bids to reach her by salmon coble. There was a delay in launching the lifeboat as the crew could not be found. In its place Lt. Rhymer of the Preventive Service rounded up a makeshift crew who performed what even by lifeboat standards must have been an outstanding rescue. Four seamen and two boys had already been brought off when James Swinny, a blacksmith, boarded the *Margaret* to try to save the elderly captain. Before he could reach him Swinny was thrown into the sea and compelled to swim back to the lifeboat. While a second attempt was being organised the captain was swept overboard. By that Sunday afternoon the vessel was a mere hulk.

Lt. Rhymer was presented with Lloyds silver medal with its representation of Ulysses for his part in the rescue. It had though another significant effect. The crew spoke enthusiastically of the seaworthy properties of the boat whereas earlier there had been reported mistrust. This may have explained the absence of the crew and the attempts to make the rescue by coble.

Sometimes little could be done but secure the cargo of a wrecked vessel. In November 1840 the forty-ton sloop *Kames* of Leith was found washed up on Spittal beach one Sunday morning. Her potato cargo was found very welcome before what remained was guarded. An oddity of this one was the insistence by Spittalers that items of ladies' clothing had been washed ashore despite the denial of any female presence aboard.

In October 1848 the Swedish vessel *Oscar den Forste* was *'brought up off the port'* after sailing from Gothenburg with a cargo of timber when with *'the sea running high she was obliged to slip her anchors and go to sea'.*

> *'Shortly afterwards she surged towards the shore, and the crew endeavoured to bring her into the port, but in this they were unsuccessful and the vessel went on the rocks about fifty yards north of the pier at twelve o'clock. In a short time both her masts went over, and before one o'clock the hull was entirely broken up, and the materials and her cargo floated about in fragments. So soon as she struck the lifeboat put off from Spittal, and by her four of the crew were rescued, the other two seamen gained the shore by their own boats.'*

The lifeboat was congratulated on its *'prompt and praiseworthy action'*. There was though growing dissatisfaction behind the scenes. In 1853 subscribers refused further contributions until the accounts were published. This could hardly have been worse timed as the previous October the decision had been taken to replace rather than repair the existing lifeboat. When the accounts were belatedly printed they were found to be in order, an unseemly reticence being the only failing of the Treasurer who stepped down to be replaced by Robert Ramsey.

In January 1853 the boat made its last rescue. The schooner *Gleaner* had left Berwick for Hartlepool but been forced to turn back after losing its bowsprit in high seas.

> *'The sea on the bar was too heavy to admit of any pilot going off to her, and the crew on their own knowledge of the place, aided by the gestures of some pilots on the pier, ventured to take the port. When nearly opposite the pier end a heavy sea struck the vessel carrying her much too far to the south. Other seas succeeding, they, together with the ebbing tide, carried her to Spittal Point, where grounding on the Colt Bat, she stuck hard and fast. The sea made numerous breeches over her, and the utmost alarm was excited for the crew who were seen to take to the rigging and make appeals for relief. The beach at Spittal was thronged with the inhabitants of the village, and every disposition and anxiety was evinced to render the utmost assistance.'*

The lifeboat crew though reckoned that the situation looked more desperate than it was. Despite the seas washing over her she showed no signs of breaking up and her cargo of pig iron was keeping her steadily upright. The tide ebbing, it was thought easier to effect a rescue if the attempt was delayed for a while. They were proved right. Not only were the seamen rescued but their clothes were brought off as well.

By now though the lifeboat was in a *'ruinous state'*. The two trips needed to bring off the *Gleaner's* crew and belongings had required constant baling and it was clearly unfit for any further service.

By this time the steersman, Andrew Davidson, had taken part in eight rescues and helped to save thirty-two lives. He and the fisherman John Wilks had been part of the crew that carried out the rescue from the *Margaret* in 1837. Doctors too were already active at sea. In 1855 Dr. Cahill was awarded the R.N.L.I. Silver Medal for his part in saving the lives of a couple adrift in an open boat in a heavy sea.

The following crewed the lifeboat:

Oscar den Forste (1848)
Prideaux Patterson, Francis Elliott, John Wood, James Johnston, Joseph Swan, John Moise.

The Gleaner (1853)
Andrew Davidson (steersman), William Lough, George Wood,
John Roughead, Robert Havery (Jun.), Alexander Patterson,
Richard Wood, Prideaux Patterson, John Wilks.

       *   *   *   *   *   *   *

A new boat being now essential, there were hopes that the Fourth Duke of Northumberland might be able to help. As Lord Algernon Percy he had seen action as a naval captain in the latter stages of the Napoleonic Wars being present at the blockade of Toulon. With peace in 1815, and still only in his early twenties, he left active service but continued to rise on the reserve list, becoming a full admiral in 1862, three years before his death.

He retained a keen interest in naval affairs, becoming First Lord of the Admiralty in 1852 and strongly backed the lifeboat cause. At the Great Exhibition he offered a prize of a hundred guineas for the best lifeboat design, encouraging the analysis and experiment that was to lead to the invention of the self-righting boat. The following year he offered Northumberland five lifeboats, leaving the Admiralty's Captain Washington to select the stations. Beyond this the Duke established schools on his lands for the children of fishermen and engaged a swimming instructor to teach fishermen to swim. He also gave a thousand bottles of sherry to the Seaman's Hospital aboard the *Dreadnought*.

       *   *   *   *   *   *   *

The Spittal station did not though benefit from the Duke's liberality and attention turned towards the R.N.L.I, as The Royal Society for the Preservation of Life had now become. After 1854 this was the only source of help. Until then The Shipwrecked Mariners' Society had had a number of boats but in that year they were handed over to the R.N.L.I, and it then concentrated on supporting the bereaved, giving shipwrecked sailors the fare home, and other charitable works.

The benefits of direction by the R.N.L.I, were that it would meet half the cost of a boat, help to pay for maintenance so long as the station made a contribution, and pay the crew. In 1855 a new boat was under construction at an estimated cost of one hundred and seventy pounds. This was a more substantial boat, thirty-six feet long with twelve double-banked oars. A particular feature were the raised air cases placed fore and aft.

The boat was called out in late March 1857, when the *Heinrich Gerdes*

Mooy, travelling from Rostock to Leith with wheat, looked about to try to cross the bar with the tide almost at low water.

> *'On Sunday afternoon, during a heavy gale from the north-east a vessel was discovered in the Bay in a dangerous position, being apparently driving upon Spittal Point. About six o'clock she went ashore at the above place and immediately filled with water…. The lifeboat immediately proceeded to her assistance and succeeded in rescuing the crew, who dropped into the boat one after the other from the bowsprit.'*

The mate had a narrow escape, falling into the sea and being carried some distance away before being rescued. The lifeboat was a full hour at sea.

In June 1858 Captain Robertson, Surveyor-General from the Board of Trade, came to inspect the lifeboat and put to sea in her. He judged the boat to be in good condition but found serious fault with the shore arrangements. Using four horses it had taken half an hour to launch the boat. He wanted the boat to be housed much nearer to its launch point. The following February the R.N.L.I. supplied a lifeboat carriage and in October 1859 a new lifeboat house was being built. The boat was thought a success despite *'low funds and deficient means.'*

Presumably the house was still being built when the crew was required to put to sea in conditions of the greatest severity at the end of that October.

> *'On Tuesday night and during the whole of Wednesday the wind blew a complete hurricane, the sea running as high as we ever remember to have seen it, and the rain descending in unbroken torrents. Dawn on Wednesday morning revealed the action of the waves, showing a small vessel broken from its moorings in the river, and thrown upon the beach. Another small vessel, coal-laden, was thrown upon the beach at Spittal; her mast soon went by the board, and she is now broken up.'*

The second vessel was the *John and Janet* of Dundee whose crew needed no rescuing for their boat was *'thrown so high on the beach that the crew experienced little difficulty in saving themselves'.*

Despite the extremity of the weather many vessels were seen passing through the Bay during that Wednesday and a sharp lookout was kept. Then –

> *'At mid-day on Wednesday, a Scotch schooner attempted to take*

the harbour, and succeeded in getting to the pier-head, where she maintained her way for nearly half-an-hour.'

Assistance should have come from the Harbour Commissioners' tug but it was still at its moorings when the vessel, the *Majestic* of Dundee, was beaten back out to sea where it dropped anchor. The lifeboat then set off to save the crew belatedly followed by the steamer. Through cold and fatigue the *Majestic's* crew was unable to slip the cable and the vessel had to be abandoned, the lifeboat bringing the crew ashore *'amidst a blinding storm of rain and surf.'*

The *Majestic* quickly dragged her anchor and was cast up on Spittal beach. There was praise for the lifeboat but criticism of the tug's dilatoriness.

*   *   *   *   *   *   *

All round the coast the storm of October 26th and 27th produced a catalogue of disasters. Forty-five ships were driven ashore at Hartlepool. Among the numerous incidents the Pilot of Milford Haven tried to enter Dover Harbour but struck the pier and was smashed to pieces with the loss of three lives and a Liverpool pilot boat sank with the loss of all hands. But the biggest shock was the loss of the *Royal Charter.*

The *Royal Charter* had been built four years ago, was an iron vessel of 2,719 tons register, and screw driven. She had been two months on passage from Melbourne. She had landed thirteen passengers at Queenstown, taken on eleven riggers off Cardiff, and sailed on with 498 persons on board. At 6 o'clock on the evening of October 26th she was brought up off Point Lynas on the northern coast of Anglesey in a violent gale. Captain Taylor fired signal rockets in the hope of attracting a pilot but none appeared and he let go both anchors. But as the gale increased to a hurricane the chains parted, the screw was fouled and the vessel drifted inexorably towards the shore, striking the rocks in four fathoms of water. A Portuguese sailor volunteered to get a rope ashore and succeeded but there was no time to deploy this lifeline.

'One tremendous wave came after another, playing with the Royal Charter like a toy, and swinging her about on the rocks. She divided amidships, and well nigh all on board were swept into the furious sea. A few minutes afterwards she also parted at the forehatch, and then there was an end. Those who were not killed by the sea were killed by the breaking up of the ship.'

There were a mere thirty-nine survivors. One recalled the moment of the disaster.

'When the vessel broke, an awful shriek – the death cry of hundreds – was heard above the violence of the storm.'

Lloyds reckoned this to have been the worst storm for twenty years. It had left 96 total wrecks while a further 530 vessels were either stranded or damaged. The loss of life was put at about six hundred.

Tweed and *Teviot*, the Berwick Shipping Company's clippers, were both at sea during the height of the storm. The *Tweed*, en route to London, saw a large nearby vessel founder and sink, the conditions making assistance impossible. Of other Berwick ships the *British Queen* found shelter near Boston while the sloop *Crane* was wrecked off Bangor but the crew saved.

A fortnight later, with the other two vessels on Spittal beach now largely broken up and Spittal people making off with the pieces, the lifeboat crew had again to be rounded up for a rescue that followed a familiar sequence. The *New Astley* from Seaham, another coaler, tried to take the bar in a rough sea but was driven on to Spittal beach. The lifeboat was promptly launched and her five-man crew safely brought ashore. The lifeboat crew was strikingly successful during this turbulent winter.

* * * * * * *

The R.N.L.I. gave seven pounds to the fourteen men who'd rescued the crew of the *New Astley* while the National Shipwrecked Institution gave ten shillings to each of the men who'd been out to the *Majestic*.

Payments to crews – by November 1861 £2,133 had been paid out – were though putting the R.N.L.I.'s resources under strain. There was too substantial investment in improving the boats. Its latest model was self-righting with a self-discharge of water. Scarborough was given one of these constructed at a cost of £315.

Additional funds were needed to sustain the scale of the R.N.L.I.'s operation. In 1862 it had one hundred and fifteen boats, each costing about forty pounds to keep up, of which eighteen were stationed in the north-east. It also faced heavy contingency expenditure. Two months after launch the new Scarborough boat was smashed against a harbour wall. An appeal was made to the people of Northumberland for contributions. One response was a collection of ten guineas from the Parish Church.

In the period 1824-1862 the R.N.L.I. saved 12,600 lives, including 700 since the start of the 1860's. During that time it awarded 85 gold and 711 silver medals.

*　　*　　*　　*　　*　　*　　*

Other measures were taken to assist seafarers. To guide fishermen the Chapel rang its bell on foggy nights and ships in harbour occasionally fired their guns as extra directional aids. As back-up to the lifeboat the Coastguards practised with Dunnett's Rocket Apparatus which they'd had since at least the 1830's. It was not particularly effective at this time, difficulty being found in getting the line to carry to a foundering vessel. But belief and perseverance were to pay off later when it played a key role in a number of rescues.

In August 1848 about a hundred fishermen drowned during severe gales and 124 boats were either wrecked or damaged. Spittal avoided harm, the worst of the storm being further north. The scale of the devastation prompted the appointment of Captain Washington to report on the state of East Coast harbours. Among his recommendations were the conspicuous placement of a barometer in every harbour, the proper lighting and dredging of harbour entrances, and the use of decked vessels. Overall he considered fishermen got a poor deal, receiving little return for their harbour dues. Berwick at this time lacked its own tide tables, being dependent on information from other ports.

Whether a great deal could be hoped for from the Harbour Commissioners was though doubtful. This secretive, self-selecting body was accused of scant knowledge of shipping and of proper employment practice.

8 The lure of the steamer

There was a growing conviction among shipping companies that the future lay with steam. It took visible shape with startling suddenness. There can never again have been so many steamships working out of Berwick as there were in 1838.

The *City of Edinburgh* had been the first arrival the previous year but wasn't around for long. She did have a proper gangway, something that assumed significance when a lady plunged into the sea while trying to board the *Ardincaple*.

The *Ardincaple* was one of two vessels purchased by The General Shipping Company. Built in 1826 and described by the company as *'a fine fast sailing steamer'* she was a robust vessel which had survived a fearful storm off Bamburghshire in 1833 in which three seamen and two ladies had been washed overboard. She must have been fairly substantial too as she often carried more than a hundred passengers and could accommodate fifty diners at a single sitting. Under various owners it was to trade with Newcastle for the best part of a decade.

The same year, 1838, the company acquired the *Glenalbyn,* which it termed *'a powerful and elegant steamship'*, primarily to conduct the Hull trade but also to have reserve capacity.

But by the end of her first season's running it was clear that she was an expensive mistake. The three-year old vessel had cost £5,700 - the cost of a new steamer was reckoned to be about £8,000. Yet from the start she was a failure on the Hull route, unable to generate sufficient trade in goods or passengers. The Hull trade had been highly profitable with the company's sailing ships doing such substantial trade in wool that the two vessels on the route were sometimes increased to three. There was a knock-on effect. The sailing vessels were transferred to less productive assignments.

The mood of thrusting optimism had been quickly replaced by a more realistic appraisal and the chairman's annual reports mulled gloomily over the problems of steam. (These were always written on the notepaper of a Berwick Inn, suggesting that the chairman clocked in early to write his report for the annual meeting – those of the Berwick Shipping Company were contained in bound volumes crammed with items of other business).

It seemed that steamships had to operate at or near to maximum capacity in order to pay. They could incur heavy expenses: soon after she was acquired the *Ardincaple* needed new boilers. They were very costly to insure and sometimes weren't. Traffic had increased but not enough. There was an *'inadequate return for the amount of capital employed'*. Nor was the company helped by the trade depression in Newcastle. It was decided to sell the *Glenalbyn* at the end of her first season.

Competition for business quickly assumed an intensive rivalry reminiscent of the railway races to the north at the end of the century with vessels at times almost literally jostling for position.

In that same hyperactive year of 1838 the *Tourist* returned to Berwick and tied up in the *Glenalbyn's* berth. The Harbour Master shouted to the captain to move. The captain refused. The Harbour Master then withdrew but returned with an axe with with he slashed the *Tourist's* moorings. Still the captain refused to move. The *Tourist's* owners, The General Steam Navigation Company then took the Harbour Master to court where the magistrates, having heard his explanation of how he'd allocated berths with regard to the varying draughts of the vessels using the port, found in his favour and fined the company.

The Berwick Shipping Company also held that steam would *'ultimately prevail'*, and brought the *Manchester* to Berwick from The Clyde. It arrived with the cachet of *'having recently conveyed from this country to Portugal the young Prince of Lieuchtenberg, first husband of Donna Maria'* and began a routine of sailing to London every ten days or so.

It too tangled with the *Tourist* in attempts to maximise trade by gaining a time advantage. Cargo handling was sometimes done at night. Something of a racing mentality developed with progress reports and passage times being printed in the papers. The *Manchester* was thought to have got the record when it completed the passage in thirty-five and a half hours.

The Berwick Shipping Company too came to consider a second vessel essential and bought the *'elegantly fitted up steamship' Rapid* which it also put on the London route.

Yet just as with the General Shipping Company the initial confidence didn't last long and the chairman's 1840 report chronicled at length the grim particulars of a year in which *'events of a disastrous nature'* meant that *'the steam trade had been carried on to little or no advantage whatever'*.

The previous year the *Manchester* had been in collision with the forty-ton *Trotter* on a foggy day in the Thames Estuary. The *Manchester*, proceeding at full speed, had hailed the *Trotter* but been unable to get any response from the single man on the *Trotter's* deck. Then it ran down and sank a sloop off Shields. On separate occasions *Manchester* and *Rapid* both swamped coal-carrying Thames barges, both belonging to the same owner who brought an action against the company and won damages. But the most serious affair was the collision with the barque *Tyrian* off Gravesend in which four of its crew were killed. It was raised only with the greatest difficulty and found to be far more seriously damaged than first thought. The *Manchester's* Captain Polwart was acquitted of manslaughter and though a further charge was laid before the Court of Queen's Bench the case was settled out of court the following year. It seems as though the emphasis on speed may have had something to do with the *Manchester's* mishaps.

There had been other problems. The *Manchester* had been damaged by a storm in the Thames and her boilers had been found defective at the height of the season. Profitably redeploying sailing vessels was difficult: the smacks were converted to sloops to save money. Then the company's argument that regularity of service justified the premium freight rates (some 20-25% above those quoted for sailing vessels) was not swallowed by all potential customers.

Underlying all reckoning was awareness of the ever advancing railways and of the threat they were bound to pose to the Newcastle and London traffic. No doubt thinking that things could only get worse the General Shipping Company threw in the towel, sold the *Ardincaple* cheaply to The Berwick Shipping Company, and opted out of steam.

The latter company had one substantial advantage in its ownership of substantial salmon fisheries, recently much increased. Though it had itself lost a huge sum (£3,469) in the collapse of the Tweed Bank it seized the opportunity of bankrupts' fisheries coming on to the market to raise a guarantee fund with which to purchase some eight thousand pounds worth of additional holdings including one-half of Sandstell and an eighth of Hallowstell.

Yet by 1843 The Berwick Shipping Company was wondering whether it might not do better with fast sailing vessels. The *Manchester's* hull and machinery had needed repair, *Rapid* had required overhaul, and then a separate fund had been set up to cope with the expenses likely to be incurred by boilers and insurance. The following year the *Ardincaple* was sold to the Tweedmouth Steamboat Company, another player in this costly game - this seems to have been its only vessel.

Details published during August 1844 give an idea of the steamers' trade. *Manchester* left with twenty-six passengers and four hundred and eighty boxes of salmon while *Rapid* returned with thirty-three passengers after a forty-hour trip.

Rapid's return in November was to be more terminal. It reached Berwick on a Monday afternoon early in the month after its last voyage of the season. Steamers weren't risked in the worst of the winter to avoid storm damage and when there was in any case less trade. The fires were drawn off, the cargo discharged, and the seamen left the vessel on the Tuesday afternoon to be followed a few hours later by the engineers and firemen, who had been cleaning the machinery, and by the captain. Between 9.00 and 10.00 o'clock there was a gathering in the main cabin, presumably a brief end-of-season celebration, then all left without noticing anything amiss.

It was a seaman on watch aboard the cutter *Mermaid* lying at the Carr Rock who first noticed the spurt of flame from the *Rapid* but it was shortly after spotted by the watchman on the man-o'-war *Skylark* and by the quay watchman. Both ships rang their bells, then the town fire bell joined in, and there was a general bestirring of residents to see what was amiss.

Mermaid and *Skylark* each depatched parties of about a dozen men, the latter armed with Heral's Patent Fire Engine, and the Corporation's engine appeared on the scene. There was considerable difficulty in getting to the heart of the fire which had been traced to the engine room. Holes were made in her decks through which water was poured while Gowan, the Berwick shipbuilder, pierced a side in order to scuttle her.

By 4.30 a.m. she was sinking fast and around 5.00 a.m., with her decks awash, all were ordered ashore. Shortly after, under the gaze of a considerable crowd, she sank in sixteen feet of water. The only casualty had been the mate who fell through the hole cut in the deck but he was retrieved without serious hurt.

At low water she presented a grim, blackened sight but closer inspection showed that though there was little left of the bridge the cabins, hold, and deck furnishings were largely intact. The initial estimate of a thousand pounds to repair the damage was revised downwards to four hundred and twenty pounds.

It turned out however that despite the frequent talk of insurance the vessel was uninsured. The accident, for such it was generally thought to be, may have been seen by the Berwick Shipping Company as providing an opportune moment for it to reduce its steamship commitment. In the event, no more was heard of the *Rapid*.

The winter break in steamship travel came as a relief to some. Fishermen claimed that they damaged or even destroyed their nets while residents objected to the practice steamers had of firing guns on entering or leaving port, particularly trying at night.

* * * * * * *

In the summer of 1845 the remaining steamers, *Ardincaple, Manchester,* and *Eclipse* tried to boost passenger numbers by advertising their regular sailings as pleasure trips and by reducing fares.

It was the completion of the North British line though that greatly increased the Newcastle trade. Now it was possible to travel from Newcastle to Edinburgh by steamer and railway for less than six shillings. In September 1846, *Eclipse* and *Ardincaple* arrived from Newcastle with two hundred and fifty passengers between them.

It was clear however that the steamers were enjoying an Indian summer and that this prosperous phase would come to an abrupt end with the completion of the Newcastle line.

Soon after through-running on the line had been achieved the *Ardincaple* was sold for the meagre sum of £255. It had been around for nine years and though it had been in collisions off North Shields the previous year was generally thought to be a lucky vessel. She'd negotiated the Tyne waters without the *Manchester's* mishaps in the Thames and was given an affectionate obituary.

In May 1848, the Berwick Shipping Company was advertising its *'new and fast-sailing clipper schooners',* Thames, Tweed, and *Commerce.* The following month it took possession of the schooner *Teviot* built by Gowan and finished with steam by sending the *Manchester* to the breaker's yard.

The *Eclipse* was withdrawn from service early in September 1848, supposedly being laid off for the winter. It was suspiciously early to be doing this though and proved to be the end of the *Eclipse* at Berwick and, for a while, of steam altogether.

9 The drowning of the Roughead brothers and loss of a pilot boat

An *'Old Fisherman'*, writing soon after the Eyemouth disaster of 1881, recalled the loss of all but one of Spittal's boats in a storm and dated this calamity to about 1770.

Jackson also mentions the drowning of four brothers. These were John, Joseph, Benjamin, and William Roughead, all in their twenties, as was William Octon, a cousin who was with them.

On Christmas Day, 1860, they had been fishing on the Dogger Bank and seem to have reached the mouth of the river about 9.00pm. though some witnesses thought it later. Though there was moonlight on land the river was shrouded in mist and full of ice floes.

Cries were heard. John Hall, a fisherman, became aware of *'a roaring from the sea'*. Alarm must have spread quickly as a crowd gathered on Spittal Point. Across the Tweed, Mr. Wilson, the Lighthouse Keeper, had also heard something and been sufficiently concerned to walk the length of the pier but been unable to make anything out. John Roughead, the boys' father, told John Hall that he thought the cries were coming from the steamer but soon had darker forebodings.

His later evidence is best given in full.

> *'I was at the beach a little before nine o'clock on Christmas Night, and there saw Prideaux Emery. Shortly after leaving him I heard cries. I ran up to the village, where I saw my wife, and told her I believed the boat was ashore and immediately ran over to Berwick for the steamer. I did not like the cries, but I did not speak to any of the Spittal people about them. I thought it would be the quickest plan to go for the steamer. I ran to the jetty, and hailed her, and immediately informed a fireman or engineer that my boat was either on the rocks or batt, and that he must get his steam up and go at once. I told him I would go to the lighthouse, and get aboard there. The man told me that Ferguson, the master, was not on board, and asked me if I knew where he lived. I said I did not know, but told him he might go himself and get him while the steam was getting up. I did not know if there was any other person on board but the man I was speaking to. I*

then ran to the pier, going along the wall from Beveridge's Stairs. When I reached the lighthouse I called out and was answered from the boat. I told them to keep their heads up, for the steamer would soon be at them. Mr. Wilson, lighthouse keeper, then desired me again to go for the steamer. I met Ferguson with two boys between the Malthouse and the Ness-Gate. I asked him why he had not got up his steam and gone to help. He swore at me, and asked how did I know where the boat was. He also asked who was to pay him. I told him I would pay him. He asked me who was to insure his boat. I said I had nothing to do with that. I offered to go with him, but he said he wanted none of my help. He told me he would pay my head all the way to Spittal. I left him at the Ness-Gate, and ran to Spittal. I then went to Robert Thews, the manager – or coxswain of the lifeboat – and rapped both at his door and window, and called out, but got no answer. I then ran to the Low Corner, where I found a number of women and some men – Thomas Hall was one of them. I then urged them to get a boat off, but they did not do it. I was then so done out that I had to be led home.'

The boat was found the following morning on Spittal Point with its mast erect and anchor thrown out. It was thought the boat's timbers had been pierced by a floe - there was a large hole on the port side of the keel. Of the men there was no sign.

In its next issue The *Berwick Advertiser* was severely critical asking how it could be that *'five men have been mysteriously and, without an effort made to save them, deprived of life'.* Why did neither steamer nor lifeboat put out to try to save them? Nor did the weather seem a sufficient reason for inaction for *'the river, though bearing numerous floes of ice, was not particularly difficult or dangerous if taken by a large boat....'*

After hearing the evidence given at an inquest at The Pitman's Arms it took a more subdued tone. John Hall recalled meeting John Roughead *'Very much agitated and running about from place to place'* but said, *'I was not aware of any danger, or I would have got a boat.'* Prideaux Emery did try to launch a boat but was driven back by the ice. Yet he reckoned a boat could have been launched from the Point if need be but didn't think there was any danger.

The inquest cleared the lifeboatmen of blame, they all said to have been at home and unaware of the tragedy until the following morning. Ferguson, though he admitted speaking roughly to John Roughead (he claimed bad language was used to him, hardly surprising in the circumstances) was also found blameless.

Some of the statements seem hard to reconcile. A coastguard witness referred to a crowd on the Point but the lifeboatmen knew nothing till the next day. There was an attempt to launch a boat but denial of any sense of danger. Yet there was great uncertainty. No-one had seen anything. Perhaps the voices weren't coming from the sea but were drifting over from Berwick as John Roughead first thought. He was the only one who knew roughly where his sons were as he'd heard their voices but may quickly have become too frenzied to put a cogent case for a rescue attempt. In any case, it may by then have been too late.

*   *   *   *   *   *   *

The feeling that more could have been done seemed to persist. The report of a later disaster was prefaced by the statement that two years ago five fishermen lost their lives *'almost at their very doors'* without any attempt at rescue.

This one too claimed five lives. About 5.00 a.m. on a Sunday morning in November 1862 a vessel was sighted and four pilot boats put out to gain her custom. During the race to reach her one of the boats *'was seen as if to lower its sail and disappear'*. No particular notice was taken. It was assumed it had given up the chase, perhaps having decided the vessel was not bound for Berwick. Later it was thought to have gone on to Holy Island to wait for one of the Berwick Shipping Company's clippers.

Eventually it had to be accepted that the boat had foundered. Three members of the Woods family and two of the related Wilks family were drowned.

Once again a relief committee had to undertake the doleful task of raising subscriptions for the bereaved.

10 The business world of Robert Guthrie

In 1838 a man who was to boost its sluggish economy appeared on the Spittal scene. This was Robert Guthrie who was to set up the Iron Foundry. He must have grown familiar since his youth with the clamour and techniques of the industry as practised by Robertson and Guthrie of Tweedmouth. Now, at the age of twenty-two, he was branching out on his own.

*   *   *   *   *   *   *

Spittal was much in need of such an initiative. The population had grown steadily from an estimated 1,330 in 1801 to 1,910 in 1831 but by 1841, on the first occasion that Spittal was enumerated separately, this had shrunk to 1,631. Berwick and Tweedmouth experienced the same trend but the Rev. William Whitehouse, writing a decade later, thought Spittal's plight particularly grim.

'We have here a greater proportion than I have seen or heard of in any village, of very aged, infirm, lame, maimed, drunken, dissolute and very poor persons. This is occasioned by the consequence of former smuggling practices, the Sabbath desecration of the pilots and their families, the bondage system of the neighbouring monstrous large farms.... whose labourers when aged are not allowed a habitation on the lands on which were spent their strength and sweat, and they come here to occupy our many miserable hovels, to enjoy their starvation parish allowance; the disasters on the seas, and the neighbouring collieries, producing many poor widows and orphans ..... Almost all young females and youths leave us for domestic service and employment in distant parts, or on the devouring sea.'

'*The inhabitants are mostly pitmen, red and white fishers*' stated the chattily informative 1806 Directory. These remained the predominant industries, the 1841 census showing that of the 372 people then employed there were 94 fishermen and 51 miners. The next largest group was that of 43 servants.

A number of industries had come and gone. Joseph Davidson had manufactured '*blues*', a product used in the chemical industry but by 1808 its deserted premises were up for sale. More recently the Greenland Yard had ceased producing whale oil after the sale of the Norfolk. This though must have afforded only very temporary employment for most, the oil often being on sale within weeks of the whaler's return. Seasonal too was the herring trade though the white fishing continued at other times while proprietors of lodging houses often sought another role, principally that of being shopkeepers, to tide them over the winter months.

The general depression of the 1830's meant though that Guthrie faced a stiff challenge.

*   *   *   *   *   *   *

He acquired a site corresponding fairly closely to the present school and playing field. Running along Main Street on one side the sizeable premises were surrounded on the other three by waste land. The area known as The Pond may have been drained before building work began.

By September 1838 Guthrie was making test castings and soon after was fully operational. Three years later he was employing some eighty to ninety men, on one occasion loading the schooner *Leith* with some one hundred and seventy tons of iron with articles ranging from twelve hundred weight to a few pounds, the largest such export yet from Berwick port. Earlier in 1841 The Foundry had despatched one hundred and twenty-three tons.

In view of the size of the labour force it is surprising that so few, a mere fourteen, came from Spittal. As any outsiders recruited and lodged in Spittal would have been included in this census figure it seems probable that he recruited from Tweedmouth workers with experience of the process.

The work, especially that of the moulder, was highly skilled with a heavy emphasis on getting a task right the first time. This required judgement and split-second timing in the midst of the crashing din and furnace heat. of the works. The two dozen labourers then living in Spittal may have been thought to have lacked skill or aptitude though some of course may have disdained the works. The exodus of youth, as noted by the Rev.William Whitehouse, must also have been a significant factor.

Beyond The Foundry Guthrie took a keen interest in Spittal affairs, campaigning against the additional penny charge on Spittal mail, supporting the new school, and becoming elected as Town Councillor for the South Ward.

In this latter capacity he raised the matter of harbour dues, an important item in his business costs. He submitted a report to the Council the burden of which was that there was no discernible principle or logic behind the scale of charges. The *Berwick Advertiser* had a look at the list of dues and concurred, congratulating Guthrie on *'a most business-like production'*. The Commissioners though could not be blamed for this as the charges were fixed by statute but must have had their own reasons for allowing the eighteen members required by statute to fall to eight.

＊　　＊　　＊　　＊　　＊　　＊　　＊

Tempers occasionally flared in the heat of The Foundry. In May 1840, Henry Lindsay took Guthrie to court for assault, a charge which was dismissed. A few months later however he lost when failing to appear to defend a complaint by Alder Beveridge of a shortfall in his wages.

This was the type of case, revolving as it did around unambiguous fact, in which employees met with a fair measure of success in court. More usually though it was the worker who faced the charge. In 1839 Guthrie took four apprentices to court expressing dissatisfaction with their work and had money deducted from their wages.

There was nothing unusual in Guthrie's conduct. Employers regularly took recalcitrant workers to court, especially apprentices. A breach of a working contract was regarded as immediately actionable as smashing a window or brawling in public even where there was no local connection. A seaman refusing to rejoin the sloop *The William Bather* on its passage from Grangemouth to Poole was sent to the House of Correction for three weeks. Once embarked on court action was best pursued with some rigour. Alexander Alexander, Herring Curer, acted against James Swinhoe and William Trotter for deserting his service but then offered to settle out of court. The two agreed to return but failed to show up. When Alexander returned to court the agreement he'd made with them was found to be wanting, the terms of engagement *'not sufficient'* and the two were at liberty. Other methods could be used to recover absconded workers. The *Berwick Advertiser* carried a front page advertisement in bold type from The Percy Iron Works in Newcastle for information as to the whereabouts of one George Nicholson who may have been the young Spittaler of that name.

The unusually high incidence of such cases in the Magistrates Court in the years 1838-1841 which included a number brought by Richard Reavely at Berwick Hill Colliery and by Major Johnston at Scremerston suggest a deliberate plan to suppress with severity any fermenting unrest at a time of much Chartist excitement. The cases continued but were more spaced out afterwards. Much later, the growth of union power compelled employers to balance the advantage of a legal victory against the possibility of a walkout.

During the years 1844 and 1845 the high level of Guthrie's commercial activity must have meant many long days and perhaps some sleepless nights. A good deal of his time was taken up with two projects beyond The Foundry. While he was intimately involved with one he grappled in vain with the other.

In his report on Public Health issues in 1850, Richard Rawlinson doubted the need for more than one gas company in a borough of Berwick's size and assumed that The Berwick-upon-Tweed Gas Lighting Company, which had been supplying Berwick since 1822, had grown complacently monopolistic.

Guthrie was the prime mover behind the launch of the rival Berwick and Tweedmouth Gaslight Company. They were usually afterwards referred to as the *'new'* and *'old'* companies which seems a convenient shorthand.

Guthrie's selling points were cost and quality. As gas production costs were only a third of those of twenty years ago it ought to be possible to supply gas *'at a moderate price'*. Then the use of coal gas would produce *'a most beautiful and clear light'*. Doubters were urged to read a pamphlet entitled *'Observations of the Advantages of Coal Gas'*.

The new company went public in March 1844, and before the end of the month all its shares were sold. Taken aback, the old company nervously considered the possibility of merger.

The pace quickened. On the land which he had himself given the company Guthrie set about building the works. It was thought that a project of this scale would normally take between nine months and a year but Guthrie had the entire plant finished in two months. By September five miles of main pipes had been laid, fifty-nine Spittal houses connected, and with the capacity to supply sixty thousand cubic feet of gas a night the company began operating that month.

In 1847 the New company won a five-year contract to light Berwick. Requirements were itemised. The lighting season was deemed to run from August 1st until May 31st. Lamps were to be lit half an hour after sunset though half could be extinguished at 1.00 a.m. There was to be a fine of a shilling a night for any lamp not working though lights were not needed on full moon nights.

*   *   *   *   *   *   *

Founding the Berwick and Tweedmouth Gaslight Company had been a largely physical enterprise but the proposed Spittal to Scremerston railway was to revolve around public meetings, committees, petitions, memorials, and legal documents. Guthrie followed closely the twists and turns of this strange affair and finally felt impelled to petition The House of Commons.

A tramway had been laid along Main Street in the early years of the century as part of the operation of moving stones from Hud's Head to the jetty to ship across The Tweed to build the new pier. Later it was revived and extended to deal with coals from Scremerston but by the 1840's had lapsed into disuse.

Towards the end of 1843 Greenwich Estates came up with a scheme for a coastal railway from Greenwich Colliery to Tweedmouth. This would necessitate land appropriation and so would require an Act of Parliament.

There was immediate opposition from two quarters. The Rev. William Whitehouse got up a petition against it on safety grounds arguing that it should never have been used for coal – it had been *'improperly opened again'* – and had been the cause of the instant death of three children. One of these was the eleven-year-old son of the pitman, Robert Bruce, who was run over by a wagon in 1832. A greater hazard to children could scarce be contrived. The phrasing of the Rev. Whitehouse's statement seems to suggest that he thought the Greenwich railway would too run down Main Street though that was never the intention. The plan clearly showed the line running further east.

The other complainants were Messrs. Reavely and Paxton, lessees of Berwick Colliery who could see no reason why they should surrender land to a commercial rival. In particular they had in mind the land at Bridge End used by them as a coal depot and which they saw Greenwich taking over for the storage and sale of coal. Early in 1844, however, perhaps influenced by what seemed to be a general support for the railway, they were talking of being prepared to accept adequate compensation. It could also have been that involving the struggling Berwick Hill Colliery in any form of litigation was not an attractive idea.

The Town Council at first temporised by asking the six-man Works Committee to investigate and report. This body, which busied itself with such matters as the design of the new gaol, water filtering, street cleaning, and the siting of slaughterhouses, functions later taken over by The Urban Sanitary Authority, delivered its verdict in February 1844.

It was uniformly hostile. All Greenwich would be doing was acquiring by compulsion land which it had failed to gain by any other means and solely for the purpose of commercial gain. The line would block access to the harbour and impede developments which the Council had in mind. Greenwich would gain control of the land between high and low water. A depot selling coal at the south end of the bridge would cause an obstruction, and, more generally, the Corporation's rights as coal owners

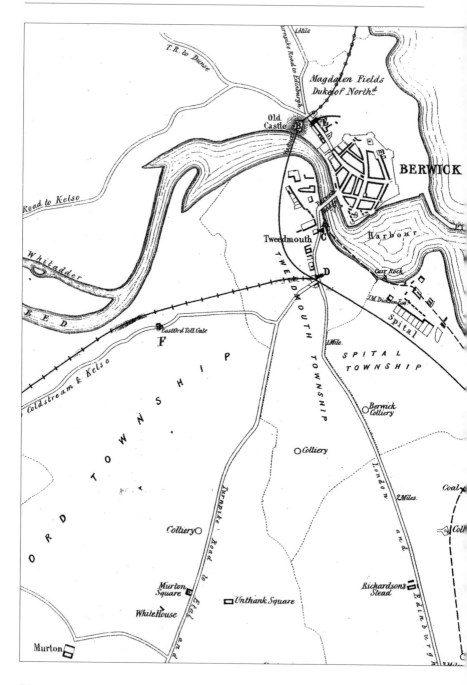

Plan
shewing the situation of the

GREENWICH COLLIERY AND OTHER COLLIERIES

NEAR BERWICK,

The Proposed Railway

FROM GREENWICH COLLIERY TO BERWICK BRIDGE,

ALSO

THE PROPOSED NEWCASTLE AND BERWICK RAILWAY,

WITH KELSO BRANCH,

(and

Adjacent Turnpike Roads.

REFERENCES.

————————	Greenwich Colliery Railway.
————————	Newcastle and Berwick Railway.
+++++++	do......do. Kelso Branch.
A	Proposed Station and Depôt of the Greenwich Colliery Railway at Berwick Bridge.
B	Proposed Station and Depôt of the Newcastle and Berwick Railway — also of the proposed Northumberland Railway.
....	Township Boundaries.
C ■	Tweedmouth Low Toll-gate. E ■ Castlegate Toll-gate
D ■	Tweedmouth High Toll-gate. E ■ East Ord Toll-gate
••••••	North British Railway.

SCALE
0   ¼   ½   ¾   1 Mile

Vachr & Sons, Lith. 29 Purliament St.

would be prejudiced. Finally, but probably significant, it was asserted that property rights would be jeopardised.

Yet the Council was not immediately swayed by these arguments and decided to reserve judgement until it had met with Mr. Bicknell, solicitor to the Greenwich Estates. Bicknell seems to have successfully calmed fears and soothed sensitivities as he apologised for the *'abrupt manner'* in which notice of the plan had been given, talked of *'misunderstandings'* and hoped they could all go forward in a *'conciliatory spirit'*. More specifically, he promised that a retaining wall would be built so that a proper road could be laid. The Council gave its agreement to the scheme provided nothing *'prejudicial to the interests of the Corporation'* was proposed. An amicable understanding appeared to have been reached.

In December 1844 the Works Committee, which now included Robert Guthrie, again reported on the railway. It had two strong objections. The railway, if built, should run no further than the Carr Rock from which point coal could perfectly well be shipped, thus avoiding obstruction of the harbour. The other related objection was to any attempt by Greenwich to gain control of the Bridge End coa depot.

These were not new arguments. As noted, the Council had heard these and other arguments against the line without any marked reaction. Yet now it found them altogether more compelling and, despite Guthrie's opposition, voted to adopt the report. The Council's earlier acceptance of the scheme had shifted through a desire to impose restrictions to outright hostility. *'The corporation dissent from the proposed undertaking'* was minuted.

*   *   *   *   *   *   *

Strangely, instead of writing to Mr. Bicknell to inform him of their current stance, the Council sent him a bundle of newspapers recording their deliberations. He was clearly taken aback and his measured prose does not conceal his annoyance. Yet Greenwich would not be deflected. *'The Corporation having passed resolutions directly opposite to their former decision, I consider it my duty to inform you that I shall get the bill introduced in the usual form.'*

Early in 1845 the Council began to campaign against the railway. In February it sent a document of protest, styled a Memorial, to the Board of Trade. In March it took advice on the framing of a petition to the House of Commons from the London solicitors, Robertson and Spottiswoode, advice that seemed to be needed, for the firm commented: *'Your petition contains some statements that are not compatible'*. The petition was despatched in April before which the Council, in a thinly attended meeting, voted by nine votes to two against the railway.

There were though many voices in favour of the Bill. The Freemen, in an April petition, saw nothing to fear from the railway. Corporation use of the tramway and depot had been guaranteed and the result was likely to be *'a better supply of coals than at present'*. Objection was taken to the Town Council opposing the Bill *'with barely enough members to form a court'* and it was held that given a vote *'a very large majority would express themselves in favour of its passing'*.

A petition of the inhabitants saw the chief gains as the building of a proper quay and the construction of a road that would shorten the journey from Berwick to Spittal by a mile. Robert Guthrie too, in his counter-petition, saw the chief advantage as *'a good hard road capable of being used at all times of the tide'*.

The *Berwick Advertiser* contrasted the Council's nine to two against the railway with the twelve hundred odd signatures on a petition in favour. It urged active support and rebutted the Council's arguments.

It was all very well for the Council to condemn the private interest of the Greenwich Estates but this body was a public trust with no motive beyond making the most of its assets. The Council with its mix of mining and landowning interests was far more likely to be swayed by private and personal motives. As for the *'long-contemplated'* harbour works – *'long indeed!'* It would seem that *'one might live beyond the age of Methuselah and see neither docks nor quays'*. (In fact there was to be a thirty-year wait). Doubt was cast on the threat supposedly aimed at Berwick Hill for the Council itself had declared that the biggest change would be brought about by main line railways. If it believed that, why the fuss about the meagre Spittal railway? The suspicion was that the defence of landed interest was the real motive behind much of the opposition.

The change of mind was the main sticking point. The Council had accepted the principle of the Bill in 1844. Why had an acceptable idea then become a bad one a year later? *'Let the majority of the Council labour as they may, and exhaust every Jesuitical skill which their ingenuity can devise,'* but no adequate answer had been given.

Greenwich, while pressing ahead with the Bill, strove to be accommodating. A draft copy was shown to the Council five months before it went to Parliament and the offer to let the Corporation use the railway was made more than once.

The precise line of the route still needed to be fixed however. With this in mind Mr. Walker, a London engineer, appeared on the scene and began discussions with interested parties. He promised to take no more land than was needed but the scale of his conception soon alarmed Greenwich. He insisted on a thirty-foot wide space between the railway and the quay wall to allow for a substantial road. Greenwich was prepared to fund a path but not a road costing some three thousand pounds which would be of no benefit to it.

The matter came to an abrupt end when Greenwich announced briefly that it was no longer going to proceed with the Bill. The following year there was mention of *the present disgraceful state of the footpath from Spittal to Tweedmouth*.

*   *   *   *   *   *   *

Whether Guthrie planned to use the gas from the new company in The Foundry or saw it as a separate business venture he would certainly have made full use of *'a good hard road'* and possibly too of the railway.

Suddenly though it ceased to matter as Guthrie went bankrupt. The Foundry closed on June 20th, 1845, a number of workers left the area, and *the failure of Mr. Guthrie'* as his bankruptcy was termed meant his immediate removal from the Town Council.

Possibly his various preoccupations had led to some neglect of his core business. Others still had confidence that this was a locally viable industry as The Tower Iron Works had started production in Tweedmouth in May.

The energetic Guthrie deserved rather better than to find his name printed in a newspaper in a list of bankrupts. He did though leave behind a name. He'd called The Foundry *The Helen Iron Works* after his wife.

11 Mining

In March 1845 a group of Unthank miners outside The Red Lion Inn (Berwick) cheered the arrival of the Union Coach, a symbol of the substance of organised labour. It bore Mr. Roberts, the miners' Advocate-General, widely known as The Pitmen's Advocate, and Mr. Daniels, editor of The Miners' Advocate.

Thomas Hepburn had pioneered union activity in the north-east. His activities attracted such powerful hostility from the owners that his union was broken and he, destitute, was forced to sign an undertaking to have nothing further to do with unions in order to find work. In 1841 a more comprehensive successor, The Miners Association of Great Britain and Ireland, was formed.

Mr. Roberts had had one striking success, the freeing from gaol of six Thornley miners on a legal technicality, but fresh in his and Mr. Daniels' minds would have been the long and bitter strike of 1844. This had seen the introduction of *'strangers'* to replace striking miners, the ejection of strikers from houses often before there were any replacements, Lord Londonderry's ban on Seaham shopkeepers having any dealings with strikers, and an attempt to suppress *The Miners Advocate*.

The men had two grievances. After their regular work men had been allowed to cut inferior coal for which they'd been paid a reduced rate. This had been stopped. Then they had complaints about one of the owners but the magistrates refused any form of legal action against him.

Mr. Roberts and Mr. Daniels *'who spoke at considerable length'*, no doubt fuelled by the contents of recent articles, outlined union concerns. There had been between two and three thousand unnecessary deaths in the last nine years in Northumberland and Durham. They argued that every pit should have at least two ventilation shafts and that charts should be kept to show old mine workings; also that it was wrong to fine men for producing damp coal when the cause was a leaking roof.

*   *   *   *   *   *   *

In the late 1830's a series of colliery disputes passed through the Magistrates Courts. Maybe the fomenting power of Chartism and awareness of militancy elsewhere in the Northumberland coalfields emboldened some of the workforce.

James Smith objected to a double-shift working pattern. But it was *'proved by the hour's man that this was an advantage rather than the reverse'.* His own preference was deemed immaterial. In another case from Berwick Hill Colliery the Spittaler John Reid showed a stubborn resolution. Set to work with three men instead of his partner who'd been taken ill *'these men said they would not take him as a partner unless he made the same allowance, which he refused to give'.* Richard Reavely, the manager, offered to pay the men who then agreed to take him but Reid still refused agreement claiming Reavely had not kept his side of the bargain.

Both men lost their cases and, by grim mischance, their lives a short while later. They were two of only five known fatalities at Berwick Hill which included a five-year-old girl caught up in machinery while taking in her father's meal.

Reavely had been prepared to acknowledge working customs and to negotiate with men up to a point. But custom was one thing and the law another. At Scremerston Major Johnston took John Hall and Peter Dickinson to court for deserting their work as pitmen. In effect they were on strike after challenging the right of masters to interfere with work down the pit or to direct changes there. The magistrates held that an owner did have such a right, the men were fined, and the pit shut down for two days in protest. The law was often used to recover absent workers. Robert Stirling and Stephen Spowart had left Scremerston claiming they were free agents but the court held otherwise.

The strongest action was taken against four Scremerston workers in August 1839. Rumours of a strike quickly spread when production ceased, suggesting something was half expected, though the reason was an engine breakdown. But there was trouble. Major Johnston had Andrew Scott, James Norris, John Richardson, and Thomas Barnes in court charged with neglecting their work and inciting others to follow their example. The first two were found guilty of trying to bring about a general strike and sent to Durham's House of Correction for two months, the other two got one month there.

The date, August 1839, was significant for it marked the height of the Chartist frenzy. The campaign for universal franchise and other political demands had been widely publicised through the medium of newspapers and passionate demonstrations took place. The Chartist leaders who thought brain more potent than brawn lost control as a wave of rioting swept through northern cities. A major demonstration in Newcastle caused alarm as it seemed to be aimed at the 'shopocracy'. The fear was more of invasion by external subversive forces than of local insurrection.

In late July the magistrates had resolved to ask the Secretary of State,

Home Department, *'for one or more companies of soldiers'.*

This was not granted but Berwick was sent a considerable armoury from Edinburgh Castle: 150 pistols with 450 flints and 4,500 cartridges along with 150 swords. At the same time between two and three hundred special constables were sworn in to bring the constabulary strength up to 372. This force was split into three companies, each set to muster on the ringing of an alarm bell. Among these special constables were the lodging house keeper and postmaster Sergeant John Mathison of *'Spittle South End'* and Sergeant John Spowart, also of *'Spittle'*.

In the event none of the weaponry was needed. All over the country Chartism subsided in the face of the huge special constabulary forces raised in the defence of property. In Berwick colliery cases and other industrial disputes less frequently came before the courts.

*   *   *   *   *   *   *

Fatalities and serious injuries did though continue to require legal process. A number of the incidents at Berwick Hill and Scremerston involved structural weakness or winding gear mishaps. In 1841 while a new pit was being dug at Berwick Hill some masons pointed out to William Chalmers a dangerous looking wall. When he walked over to examine it it gave way plunging him eighteen feet to his death. In 1847 the struggles of six men to move a large stone cracked the roof and left James Rae buried under the fallen matter. Falling stones killed two Spittalers, John Reid and George Spowart, and broke the thigh of another, Thomas Burn.

Poor light seems to have been a factor in the death of Robert Oliver at Scremerston. On his way to work a side shaft he stepped over the edge of the shaft but missed the cradle and plunged to his death. Henry Watson, in charge of the horses at Berwick Hill, survived with a broken arm and leg an accident that would today be seen as stemming from casual procedure. *'He was ascending the pit when three of the men at the pit-mouth attached themselves to the descending end of the rope: the consequence of the additional weight caused Watson to ascend with great rapidity, and with considerable violence he was jammed against the pulleys at the mouth of the pit.'*

In 1856 James Fade was drawing some cinders to warm his coffee from the Scremerston boiler when it exploded, killing him instantly and reducing the shed which housed it to fragments. Six years later a nine-year-old boy leapt from a moving wagon taking coal to the North East

Railway, missed his footing, and was crushed. A further casualty was feared that year when what looked like a body was spotted at the end of a shaft. Investigation showed this though to be the remains of a dead sheep fortuitously covered by a tarpaulin.

Bereaved wives and injured workers got little sympathy from Matthew Forster, one of Berwick's two M.P.'s. During a debate on The Mines and Collieries Bill he stated that nineteen out of twenty accidents were the men's fault. *'He had looked over the bill and did not perceive a single clause directed against the notorious carelessness of persons employed in mines and collieries.'* The bill failed to progress as did a subsequent attempt to outlaw the use of gunpowder and candles in mines.

*   *   *   *   *   *   *

On the morning of July 6th 1853 there was a gathering in The Hen and Chickens Inn. A number of those present had in mind the auction of Berwick Hill Colliery set for later that day. They would have seen the Corporation's somewhat ingenuous advertisement:

> *'This colliery is remarkable for easiness of access to its working seams and the small expense at which coals are got from it.'*

Among the party were George Carr, manager of Scremerston Colliery and timber merchant, and his Scremerston agent, Stephen Scott, who were seen talking together at the end of a room. Present too was James Sinclair, best known as an Insurance Agent – as the Lloyds man he was speedily on the scene of wrecks – but he was also manager of Berwick Hill Colliery. Ralph Aitchison, the innkeeper, later claimed to have spotted Scott and Sinclair in private conversation though others thought they kept their distance. These and other seemingly inconsequential details were to become significant later.

*   *   *   *   *   *   *

The last auction had been in 1822 when the taker had been Robert McAdam, a Spittal quarryman. By promising to put in an engine and to make the colliery viable for forty or fifty years McAdam and Mr. Redpath, a builder who turned out to be the principal investor, got the rent reduced from £265 to £150 a year. A further reduction to £100 was granted on McAdam offering to start a coal yard in the town and to *furnish good and sufficient coal to burgesses'* at a price no higher than fourpence-halfpenny a boll. This last concession may have been why he was granted a ten-year extension of the lease in 1826.

Popular though this reduced price must have been with the burgesses it can't have been too good for McAdam and Redpath as a boll was later found to cost fivepence to produce and a substantial quantity, some two-fifths of total output, was being sold on this loss-making basis. After investing about two thousand pounds in the colliery the pair went bankrupt in 1830 and thereafter the business was carried on by trustees.

Berwick Hill was a comparatively small mine. Most of Spittal's fifty-odd pitmen would have worked at Scremerston which in 1855 was employing one hundred and twenty men. By the terms of its lease Berwick Hill had to employ no fewer than four and no more than fifteen hewers. Not that this was always kept to. In December 1836 thirty-two men were working there. For this and other violations of the lease forfeiture was considered. There were also disputes over tentale rent, the payment for coal raised beyond that linked to a fixed rent. In addition, the legal validity of the inadequately documented ten-year lease extension was questioned.

John Taylor of Haswell Colliery, Durham, inspected the colliery in April 1853, and concluded that much needed doing. He found the levels in a bad state (as too did Robert Stephenson though seemingly on the basis of written evidence rather than personal inspection) and considered an updated survey overdue. He recommended an initial rent of around £100 a year to allow for the expense needed in winning new coals. The supply though he deemed ample, reckoning that the Cooper Eye seam, one of four running through the colliery, would itself sustain production for some thirty years.

The Town Council was decided on one thing. There would be no grey areas as a result of loose wording on the new lease.

*   *   *   *   *   *   *

James Gibson, auctioneer, knew who at least two of the bidders were going to be. Stephen Scott had told him that his bids were to be recognised *'by his putting his fingers in his waistcoat in a certain manner'* while James Sinclair had asked him to watch for *'his putting his pencil in his mouth'*. Also present was the same Robert McAdam who'd taken the lease more than thirty years ago. He'd brought his son, John Patrick, from Newcastle in case an unknown bidder looked advisable.

The bidding proceeded until Sinclair stepped on McAdam's foot, a prearranged signal to prevent the pair from bidding against each other, and bid £172. There was no response from Scott and the colliery was knocked down to Sinclair. That day the Town Council minuted *James Sinclair, Insurance Broker, (on behalf of Patience Johnson, Widow, John Carr, William Carr and Charles Carr) was declared the highest bidder and taker'.*

*   *   *   *   *   *   *

Although it was generally assumed that Sinclair had been acting for the Carrs a different story surfaced some weeks later when Sinclair claimed to have taken the colliery in his own name. He was insistent that he'd come to no prior arrangement with George Carr or Stephen Scott before the auction. He had though gone to Scremerston the day after the auction to meet Patience Johnson, widow of R.Johnson in whose name Scremerston was still being run. Sinclair claimed that at this meeting she'd offered him a fixed yearly sum in return for the omission of his name from the lease.

Whether that was so or not there was no further action for almost two months. Then on August 24th Sinclair wrote to Patience Johnson asking for a meeting as *'I wish to come to a definite understanding what the amount of compensation is to be otherwise the whole arrangement is at an end'.* She replied the next day, refusing to see him and denying any obligation. *'I am at a loss to understand what agreement you refer to.'* She reiterated this in another letter five days later. *'I confess I feel astonished at your now wishing to make out that you took the colliery on your own account.'* In a later affidavit she concluded that Sinclair *'had some intention to impose upon me ... but finding I was firm and would not recognise him ..... he gave the game up'.* She was wrong there though. He hadn't.

Legal wheels started turning. Robert Douglas, Sinclair's solicitor, wrote to the Town Council in early September demanding that the lease be assigned to Sinclair and threatening action should it be granted to anybody else. Faced with this George Carr started marshalling evidence to support his case.

Just as it was important for Sinclair to show that he'd been acting independently of Carr and Scott so Carr needed to show that Sinclair had been acting on his behalf. According to Carr, Sinclair met him on Hyde Hill after the auction and talked of *'our good fortune in taking the colliery'.* Later at Carr's woodyard sale he *'came to me in a bustle as he always is'* to discuss sureties and was told to return to the auction and bid for the coalyard as well, which he did successfully.

Most witnesses gave evidence that favoured Carr, asserting that Sinclair had given no sign that he'd taken the colliery on his own behalf. Some stated explicitly their desire to remain on good terms with George Carr and this desire may have coloured the substance of other testimony. For Carr's business activities had a remarkable range. As well as running Scremerston Colliery and his timber yard he'd started up Carr's Brewery (later the Tweed Brewery) in the yard of The Governor's House. From there too he sold guano, then much in demand. Alive to overseas possibilities he acted as agent for the British American Land Company and recruited workers for the St. Lawrence Canal. When Australian gold became the magnet, he commissioned a six-hundred ton vessel from Gowan the Berwick Shipbuilder. In his latter years he moved heavily into mining but suffered a downturn in fortune. It was reported in 1858 that *'his affairs became involved during the recent financial crisis'* and he sold three collieries. On his death in 1865 he left six lots of Spittal property. These included a house, shop, tenements, and 1,430 square yards of land between Main Street and the Gas Works, land described as suitable for building.

He was not a man to be lightly crossed. Even so not all the affidavit evidence went his way. The auctioneer, for instance, had no sense that Scott and Sinclair were working in tandem. *'I clearly understood from his manner and conversation he intended taking it on his own account,'* he recalled. Robert McAdam had a different stated reason for not bidding against Carr at the auction, being grateful for past kindness and content to see him get the lease.

Neither side yielding, the issue was to be resolved in the Court of Chancery in October. The Town Council, which had been a frustrated bystander, arranged to send an observer to the trial. After two deferments the case came up but was shortly after settled out of court. The Carrs got the lease so there must have been some form of trade-off. Almost certainly it was the timber yard whose wares Sinclair was shortly afterwards advertising.

*   *   *   *   *   *   *

Mr. Taylor of Haswell Colliery had advised against necessarily awarding the contract to the highest bidder. He warned of the practice of mothballing certain pits after purchase while concentrating production on the most productive source. Even then there was fierce dispute over the future of Norham's Greenlawalls pit after the owners withdrew the pumps and allowed the mine to flood.

Soon after the auction rumours began to spread that Scremerston was indeed running down Berwick Hill. Mr. Taylor, whose proposal that he inspect the mine at regular intervals had been accepted, reported that it was being effectively managed. The money passed from the old to the new tenants was being spent on the mine. The installation of a seven horsepower engine *to form a wagon way down to the full deep of the seam'* allayed fears that Johnson and Carr might satisfy themselves by working only the more easily got rise coal.

There was though lengthy discussion in the Town Council when the new tenants wanted to make the new deep winning from the Scremerston side. The two pits being part of a continuous geological whole, they were artificially separated by a reserve barrier. Permission was finally given on condition that the barrier was replaced and the tenants bear the cost.

Working through the barrier had been seen as a potential threat to the independence and integrity of Berwick Hill particularly as the same company held the leases of both mines. Indeed the Town Council's eagerness to assign the lease to Johnson & Co. seems surprising in view of the deep suspicion of Greenwich's intentions at the time of the proposed Spittal railway. Admittedly there was a difference between dealing with a rival institution and prospective tenants. But the Town Council was close to allowing Berwick Hill to be absorbed into a local monopoly with only marginal control of its operations.

12 Spittal Subscription and other schools

The Victorian age was every bit as obsessed with education as our own, seeing it as the path to advancement and a force for improved social morality. Literacy was often assessed. Prisoners in Berwick Gaol had their skills tested and results tabulated under four headings for each individual, a practice that persisted until the mid-1870's. The lack of any educational provision was seen as real deprivation. The fact that the enumerators for the 1891 Census found a surprisingly high level of literacy among the poor throughout the Borough suggests there was effective and widespread teaching both before and after the 1870 Act made education compulsory.

*   *   *   *   *   *   *

In 1837 a provisional committee was formed with the idea of establishing a school in Spittal. *'The want of the means of education of the poor and labouring classes in Spittal has long been a source of deep regret,'* it noted. The lack may have been the more keenly felt since the opening of the Tweedmouth National School in 1824 which some Spittal children attended.

The first hurdle was financial. A grant of seventy-five pounds could be claimed from the Lords of the Treasury but an equal sum had to be raised first. By early 1838 sufficient progress had been made for a site just off School Lane to be acquired and for building to begin. The British and Foreign Schools Society gave seventy-five pounds towards the building of the schoolhouse.

In November 1838 the newly-appointed *'Committee of Management'* moved on to the appointment of a schoolmaster. It had definite views on the type of teacher sought, wanting a man of drive capable of taking his pupils through a rigorous and productive course. In addition he must be of *'pious and irreproachable habits'* and aged under forty. The choice must be approved by three ministers.

The committee chose the thirty-two-year-old Ninian Redpath who had been teaching in Union Street. His wife, Maria, was the same age and they had a four-year-old son, James. From the outset the committee felt confident in the appointment. He was to be paid thirty pounds a year for three years with a rent-free schoolhouse and school wages to be fixed by him *'at a moderate rate'*. These consisted of a penny or twopence from each child and amounted to about the same as his salary.

Schooling began in February 1839. In October the first Annual Meeting of subscribers was held in the Town Hall to review progress. It heard that there had been about one hundred and thirty on the role though that had dropped to eighty-eight when the herring fishing season started.

Conscious of a forty pound debt, the management committee tried to persuade its subscribers to become annual contributors. To this end it suggested that subscribers would be interested in *'seeing the clean, neat, and orderly appearance of the children, and hearing them go through their various exercises'*. A public examination was set for the following March, Mr. Redpath and his *'eminently carried on'* system meanwhile receiving high praise.

The public examination too proved highly satisfactory. *'After prayers the children were examined ...... in reading, writing, arithmetic and scientific and religious knowledge.'* Altogether they were *'a great credit to themselves'* and did *'honour to their laborious and devoted instructor'*. Of the one hundred and fifty then on the role one hundred and forty-two had been examined, an exceptionally high proportion.

Mr. Redpath continued to receive good notices. In 1844 the committee expressed itself *'highly pleased with the exertion of the teacher'* and he remained *'very satisfactory'*. He was also active in other roles, superintending the Sabbath School and chairing temperance meetings, a cause for which he seems to have been particularly enthusiastic.

In 1847 the debt was finally paid off and the following year the school admitted its thousandth scholar. In 1849 there was an average attendance of one hundred and forty during the first three quarters with a drop to one hundred and four during the summer. The main thing though was that the pupils were *'numerous'*.

Change was though imminent. In November 1849 Mr. Redpath, whose son had now been joined by two daughters, announced his intention to emigrate.

*   *   *   *   *   *   *

The following year the twenty-eight-year-old James Kirton took up residence in the schoolhouse. He too was well regarded being quickly congratulated on his *'gratifying success'* after an examination in which his pupils answered questions with *'ease and readiness'*. These exams, conducted by the Rev. Whitehouse and the Rev. Porteous during the years they worked in tandem, covered a fair range. In 1853 the children were examined in geography, mensuration, arithmetic, writing, English grammar, and reading. In addition the advanced class *'showed a correct knowledge of scripture history.'* Mensuration, or practical mathematics as it had been termed two years earlier, must have been designed to make the subject relevant and useful. Since Mr. Redpath's first examination science had disappeared but geography and grammar been introduced.

School progress continued to be reviewed in the annual meeting at the Town Hall, generally presided over by the Mayor. Sometimes there was a reasonable attendance but on occasion few came which had a *'tendency to dishearten both teacher and pupils'*. Those who went heard that the school was in a *'thriving state'* (1853) and got a *'very gratifying report'* (1857). Of course any school looking to the generosity of subscribers and needing support from the community is bound to talk itself up to some extent.

These November meetings, at least as reported, and the reporting was often rather perfunctory, were largely concerned with practical matters, in particular finance. In 1859 though Councillor Robert Ramsey, who by now had been secretary for over a decade and who regularly rode along from his Tower Foundry Works to keep an eye on things, delivered a speech which gave a real insight into practice and expectation. After reading the treasurer's report, which showed a balance of seven pounds, eighteen shillings and sixpence he moved on to a more general account of school life,reported as follows.

> *'The secretary also read the twenty-first annual report of the committee which showed that the pupils were progressing steadily in the various branches of reading, writing, arithmetic, and geography. From Mr. Ramsey's own experience of the scholars, he could inform the meeting that some of them could read and write very well; and some of them knew a little of geography, and were able to point out the different places on the maps. It could not be expected that they could give them a great knowledge of geography, but they got a fair insight of what it was, and were able to understand what sort of a world it was they lived in, with the assistance of the maps. Some of them could read and spell well. When Mr. Ramsey visits the school he always endeavours to impress upon the scholars the importance of spelling correctly; for although they might read and write well, they might be deficient in spelling. The teacher also learns them to write well*

on slates before he allows them to write on copy-books. There could be no doubt that the teacher pays the greatest attention to the school, and spends the whole of his time in the education of his pupils. When Mr. Ramsey goes to Spittal he generally stays at least half an hour at the school, and he makes it a practice to see that all have their hands and faces clean, and their bonnets off. He would ask them who they thought was the best scholar in the school and who was the worst, but all of them would remain dumb, and he would inform them that he thought the best scholar was the one who paid the greatest attention to his lessons, and the worst scholar was he who paid no attention to them. The school, he said, was a great benefit to Spittal, the children of which village would without it lack any education whatever, while under present circumstances many of the more advanced scholars were pretty far conversant with the rudiments of education. The average attendance during the year had been fifty boys and forty-four girls – at present there were forty boys and thirty-nine girls. During the winter the attendance is much larger than during the summer, for as soon as the fine weather sets in the parents take their children from school in order to make a penny wherever that can be got. They need never look for a large attendance during the herring season. Mr. Ramsey also suggested an examination of the school annually, but not to take place later in the year than the month of April, for after that month the greater part of the children leave the school after having obtained their knowledge during the winter, and at which time they would cut a better figure at an examination.'

The committee then thanked Mr. Darling for a supply of coals. (There had been a considerable number of benefactors. Among them, Greenwich Colliery and Thomas Nesbit of Springhill had also given coals and Mr. Marjoribanks M.P. three pounds. A particularly welcome gift must have been the hundred bound copies of the Bible from Robert Guthrie.) it was resolved to take steps to get the school placed under Government Inspection and then one other matter was raised.

'The Rev. Wm. Porteous originated a long discussion respecting parties holding Sunday Schools in the school-room during divine service without first obtaining the permission of any person connected with the school, but gaining admittance by a key which they possessed. It was agreed that a new lock be supplied to

the door, and all parties wishing the school-room must first apply to the trustees.'

The significance of this will shortly be considered.

*   *   *   *   *   *   *

Looking at the closing years of the Redpath and Kirton eras there is a significant drop in attendance. The average for the three quarters before the summer exodus was one hundred and forty in 1848, ninety-four in 1859. Circumstances would seem to have favoured Kirton. There was a stronger local economy, increased population, and the two rival schools faced by Redpath had been reduced to one. Something was not quite right.

When, in January 1862, William Jackson arrived fresh from Borough Road Training College to replace James Kirton Robert Ramsey gave the pupils a 'pep talk'. He emphasised the need for regular attendance, respect for teachers, cleanliness, and orderly conduct.

As has probably now become clear, Robert Ramsey was the most actively involved member of the management committee. It did though include other influential figures such as James Wilson of the Chemical Works and George Black of The Forge.

*   *   *   *   *   *   *

Just how many children were being educated in Spittal during Jackson's boyhood seems clear enough. The 1851 census describes three hundred and forty of the four hundred and sixty-five childred aged between four and fifteen then resident in Spittal as *'scholars'*. Yet if this number really was getting a full-time education, where were they all going?

The late Cllr. Frank Swinney referred in his *'History of Spittal'* (1966) to a tradition of there having been two private schools in Spittal, one roughly on the site of the present Albion Inn, the other at 89, Main Street.

The 1841 census confirms the tradition while Jackson breathes life into the facts. Esther Lauther had stopped running her girls' school by 1851 though and its location is uncertain. Not till the 1860's did another girls' school appear. The other school was run by George Boston, Jackson's 'Dominie Bowson', who unquestionably taught on the Albion Inn site and did so for over twenty years. The lay-out of the buildings on that corner was a little different then, two rectangular blocks set at right angles not quite converging, Boston's house being number 154 and the Tweed Inn, later taken over by the Albion, number 156. Large numbers of Spittal children must have experienced his idiosyncratic methods. The eldest son of his sizeable family was Robert Boston, the future Herring King and pillar of Spittal society.

During the 1850's then George Boston's was the only other school in Spittal at a time when some two hundred more children were apparently being educated than went to Spittal School. A handful may have continued going to Tweedmouth School and there was 'Hobbie' Elliott's establishment. But to have absorbed the bulk of the two hundred George Boston's school would have had to be very large indeed, far bigger than the purpose-built school, which seems unlikely. It is probable than many were counting Sunday School.

The fuss made by the Rev. Porteous about unauthorised use of the school-room shows that there were several of these. Attendance at one of these would too meet the census definition of education – regular tuition by a master. How much time needed to be spent was unspecified as was the nature of the tuition.

The surprisingly high proportion of children listed as *'scholar'* (73% of 5-14 year-olds and 78% in the 5-12 age range) shows that most parents thought some attachment to education desirable. Some, especially those with large families, must have made sacrifices to send their children to school.

The labourer, Robert Percy, for example, had seven children. Two were then (1851) not of school age but the other five were all *'scholars'* including two boys of fifteen and sixteen. It was unusual for boys of that age not to be working and their education presumably was more than Sunday School. Families who completely spurned education were very much a minority.

It would be quite possible to believe there were three hundred and forty children in full-time education if George Jackson's *some three hundred boys and girls'* had attended Spittal School. It would all tie in rather neatly. But for some reason he inflated the figure, more than doubling the actual role.

A fortnight after Robert Ramsey's address the Rev. Porteous wrote to *The Berwick Journal* to point out that the Subscription School was not Spittal's only school as had been strongly implied. As a frequent visitor to Spittal Robert Ramsey must have known this well enough and can only have been deliberately dismissive.

13 Inns and Public Houses

In the first half of the century Spittal had some twenty Inns and Public Houses though not all at the same time. The 1806 Directory lists the Golden Fleece, The Smack, The South End, The Sheep, and The Beehive but the last three had gone by the early 1820's. During that decade there were six additions of which three, The Red Lion, The Pitmans Arms, and The Ship were to last the century though only The Red Lion survives today. The number of licensed premises rose from four in 1827 to twelve in 1855 with several, such as The Moulders Arms and The Coopers Arms having a clear trade link.

The Norfolk Arms, always oddly unlisted, could have been Jackson's thirteenth house if it was still around. There were also at least two beer houses, The Union Tavern and The Mariners Home, though the latter got a spirits licence in 1866. The Union Tavern, when Belford Brewery had it up for sale, was described as follows:

> '.... well situated for combining the beer trade with a grocery or shop of general goods being in the immediate neighbourhood of the Bathing Houses.'

These had operated under a different regime, being licensed by the Excise rather than the Magistrates. When the Magistrates got control of them in 1857 they steadily phased them out.

There was no shortage of suppliers. By the late 1840's Elliott's and Sibbitt and Dickson had ceased but Border Brewery, which was to gain control of many houses, and Carr & Co. had started up while Belford and Chirnside Breweries were also within range. Coldstream Brewery Co. offered free delivery of theirs.

Many licencees struggled. In 1843, the seventh year of its existence, the Tweed Inn was on to its third occupant. This was typical with lengthy tenancies being very much the exception. A subsidiary income was often essential. When The Bell Inn was robbed durung a September 1844 night the licensee, Mrs Wilson, and two servant girls were found to have been asleep in kitchens with the bedrooms occupied by lodgers. Many landlords had a different day job. George Carr remained a fisherman while running the Coopers Arms and Robert Hills worked as a labourer during his time at The Moulders Arms.

Two men did though have a lengthy connection with the trade. Thomas Crowther, Herring Curer, moved to The Tweed Inn after some fifteen years at The Red Lion while William Carr, cooper, took root at The Coopers Arms and, more briefly The Salmon Inn.

There were other outlets available to anyone fancying a drink. Thomas Purves had a grocer's shop next door to the United Presbyterian Chapel (the site of the present St. Paul's). An advertisement of 1858 showed that he stocked London Porter and Stout, Burton and Edinburgh Ale, British Wines, and Raspberry Vinegar. It also stated that he'd introduced a circulating library which must have provided a splendid pretext to pretend to go in for one thing and come out with something rather different. Later he sold spirits.

If you had the pocket and taste you could pay a visit to Alder & Co., Berwick wine merchants with an extensive list. At the other end of the market you could purchase a volume entitled *'How to Brew Splendid Strong Ale, at sevenpence per gallon without the usual brewing utensils'.*

✳   ✳   ✳   ✳   ✳   ✳   ✳

Whether landlords liked it or not they were de facto law enforcers. Much of the regulation came from the Magistrates. In 1837 they decreed that Beerhouses should not open before 5.00a.m. or stay open after 11.00p.m. Not surprisingly, the later time was the cause of most trouble.

Temperance lobbying, and especially agitation against Sunday drinking, occasionally prompted the Government to act. It did so in 1854 when it introduced restrictions north of the Border in the Public Houses (Scotland) Bill. This required all Public Houses to shut at 11.00p.m. and to remain closed on Sunday. Bona Fide travellers were though allowed Sunday refreshment at inns, defined as premises with more than four sleeping apartments. Among the first victims of the new law was a large party of eminent divines, dining out in Edinburgh after a day spent at the General Assembly of the Church of Scotland, unaware of the new law.

It wasn't long before the vagueness of the bona fide provision was causing problems and occupying the lawyers. How far did you have to journey to qualify? Did a man walking from Edinburgh to Portobello count?

The following year the New Beer Act repealed much of the 1854 Act while this time legislating nationally. Sunday opening hours were to be from 1-3 p.m. and 5-11 p.m. and Houses were to stay shut until 4.00 a.m. the following day. This marked a considerable retreat from the principle of total Sunday closure which many had been hoping would apply south of the Border too, and was seen as a counter-measure inspired by Brewers and Distillers.

The bona fide clause was omitted. It was though in force until comparatively recently. Older readers will recall having to log their journey in a hotel's register in order to have alcohol with their Sunday lunch.

*　　*　　*　　*　　*　　*　　*

Disregard of the Sunday trading law was the commonest cause of prosecution of the Borough's licensees. Alexander Patterson was charged with having The King's Head open at 10.40 a.m. when Police Officer Carr found three men smoking with a mug and glasses on the table. When William Crystal and Peter Dickenson were apprehended drunk one Sunday morning they said they'd been drinking at the Red Lion. Taken to court the licensee, Robert Alder, tried to shift the blame.

> *'They had had two pots of whisky in defendant's house, which they obtained from the servant, both the master and the mistress being in bed at the time. Defendant stated that the servant had got the key of the cellar from his bedside without his knowledge, and that so soon as he knew that the witnesses were in the house he got out of bed and turned them away.'*

The Magistrates though found this hard to credit, reminded him that he was in any case responsible for the acts of his servant, and fined him a pound with ten shillings costs.

'Keeping a disorderly house' was another recurring charge and one that became more frequent during the railway construction years when large numbers of navvies roamed the Borough and the Magistrates became preoccupied with maintaining order. The large number based in Spittal preferred drinking in Berwick but could make their presence felt in Spittal. Thus P.C. William Reid found it necessary to handcuff Edward Pringle and the navvy, James Coil in a Spittal Public House.

Among the locals, the Havery's caused the most trouble, and must have been greeted with watchful apprehension by landlords. Prideaux Emery complained to the Magistrates that he was 'getting a pint of beer when Havery came in and struck him'. Alexander Patterson, landlord of The King's Head, also had trouble with the Havery's. Breaking up a fight between two brothers he was struck on the shoulder by Robert Havery who later returned to smash some of his windows. On another occasion Robert Havery was apprehended in a *'drunk and riotous state'* at one o'clock on a Sunday morning, fighting and surrounded by a large crowd.

Nor was the fighting restricted to the menfolk. Christina Havery,

Robert's wife, was charged with assaulting Thomasina Patterson.

> *A female witness 'saw them tuck up their sleeves and have a regular pitched battle. Prideaux Emery, fisherman and constable of Spittal broke it up by pulling off defendant and two daughters from complainant lying underneath'.*

John Havery was sent to the Quarter Sessions to answer for a more serious assault, described by his target, Andrew Thompson, as follows.

> *'I left Carr's public house with three or four more. Swinney and I came down the street together, and when we got to the passage leading to the house occupied by Connolly, we heard a woman crying as if for help. I heard Havery speak. I knew him by his tongue. I was perfect sure it was him. He was muttering and talking. I have been brought up beside him all my life. I was finding my way into the passage and asked, "Who's there?" but nobody spoke. I got the knife into my arm then.....'*

He was stabbed four times, three slashes cutting his clothing but the fourth severing an artery. Probably only the prompt attention of Dr. Wilson saved his life. A degree of provocation was accepted on Havery's behalf but nothing like enough to justify his use of the knife, and he was sent to prison for four months with hard labour.

Henry Pickles, a Lancastrian, had problems running The Commercial Inn. Thomas Johnston, a fisherman, had had two pints of ale but when he asked for another was refused and struck Pickles in the face while being thrown out. He was later taken to court for assault. So was the joiner, William Moor, *'for an assault so serious as to cause Pickles to be confined to his house'*. William Reid, Police Officer, was called and later gave evidence in court.

> *'He found the landlord bleeding at the head and his face seriously bruised.... He had seen Mr. Morrison, surgeon, twenty minutes ago, and he said that he considered Pickles not yet out of danger.'*

He recovered in time to see Moor refused bail and jailed though perhaps thinking it more prudent to settle out of court with such a bruiser that is what he did.

Landlords faced other difficulties. Money problems too dogged Pickles. A bill from Carr's Brewery stating baldly *'1851. To balance of account £12.10.0d.'* went unpaid with the result that the Brewery took away his pass-book and sold his furniture. Carr's lawyer informed the County

Later photographs of two Spittal inns

The Red Lion is Spittal's oldest suriving Public House, known to have been in existence in 1822.

The Commercial Inn, scene of Henry Pickles' turbulent tenure.

Court that the debt reached back to 1847 but the Judge adjourned the case until the sum owed was itemised, as was legally required for amounts over five pounds.

Further detail doesn't seem to have greatly helped the Judge who appears to have wrestled with the case in vain, observing on the occasion of its third deferral that *the more he considered the case the more puzzled he was in unravelling its difficulties*. When it came to court for the fourth time Carr & Co., mindful no doubt of the ever-mounting legal bill, withdrew the case. Soon after Pickles seems to have been working as a quarryman, presumably not greatly missing the bar.

Something overwhelmed Thomas Davidson at The Ship Inn for he did a midnight flit or, as the lawyer put it, *absconded from the county taking the licence with him*. He was tracked down the following year (1851), brought back to Berwick, and taken to court for deserting his wife and children and leaving them chargeable to the parish. He was sent to the workhouse until he could find himself a job.

In September 1854 an inquest was held into the death of a four and a half-year-old boy. George Wood, a pilot's son, had got into the habit of following around a fisherman, Andrew Davidson, and had gone with him into The Bell where he'd been given whisky. Helen Dawson, the landlord's daughter, testified to refusing Davidson's call for a pot of whisky until the child had gone. But by then the damage had been done. On his first visit to the sick boy Dr.Morrison applied leeches but called back he found the boy in convulsions, shortly after which he died.

Robert Hills of The Moulders Arms found himself in court, along with his wife, as witnesses to the antics of two of his customers. The herring curer Archibald Yeoman claimed eighteen shillings and sixpence for the destruction of a coat.

The pair had been drinking in The Moulders Arms when Crystal got up to go. Earlier Crystal had been fighting and had lost a good deal of shirt sleeve. Yeoman offered to lend him his coat. Crystal accepted this but instead of wearing it home took it into the pub's kitchen where he tore it, painted it, then put it on the fire. Yeoman though lost the Judge's sympathy when it turned out that he'd made a spittoon of the landlord's hat and, with help, had similarly ruined two or three others. *'In fact, it was a drunken frolic,'* observed the Judge, dismissing the case.

The reason for the hostility became clear a few weeks later when the pair reappeared, this time with Crystal as the plaintiff. Yeoman had been using Crystal's yard to build a boat for a rent of one pound. Crystal had been putting it about Spittal that this had not been paid. Mrs Hills though testified that she'd lent Crystal a pound. Crystal, after lengthy evasion, finally admitted receiving the pound and giving it to Yeoman as compensation for the destroyed coat. The Judge had now heard more than enough. *'Drunken swabs altogether,'* he exclaimed, dismissing this case too. *'The whole party seems to have been in that disgracefully drunken state so common in our heighbourhood......'*

*   *   *   *   *   *   *

A temperance lecturer, Mr.Hedley, petitioned the magistrates for a ban on Sunday drinking, claiming some Public Houses never shut on Saturday nights. Exaggeration this may have been but the recorded times of police visits showed that some at least kept very late nights.

In 1854 the Mayor informed the Town Council of a petition from Spittal. This complained of Saturday night drinking lasting noisily until three or four o'clock on Sunday morning. He thought the nuisance real, excepting only Carr's and Crowther's houses (The Coopers Arms and The Tweed Inn).This was not a new complaint. Alderman Bogue said that when Mayor he'd received similar petitions. Asked his opinion, Councillor Crowther, in what seems a rather diplomatic response, said he knew nothing about it as he always went to bed early.

Arguments against intemperance were both moral and practical. People going to church objected to having to negotiate their way past drunks and to other unwanted encounters. There was too the more altruistic sense of wasted lives. At the same time there were general financial implications. Part of the increase in the general rate was put down to drunken pauperism. Some thought it accounted for as much as three-quarters of the Poor Rate. Moreover, a good deal of crime, some reckoned as much as half, was thought to have been fuelled by drink.

One proposed remedy was a reduction in the number of Public Houses. When compared with other towns Berwick did seem to be liberally supplied. For instance , Manchester had one house for every 754 people, Newcastle one for 251, but Berwick one for every 188.

The argument that supply created demand had earlier been challenged by the radical M.P. Joseph Hume. If so, he asked, why weren't some continental countries where spirits were a quarter or a third of the British price *'sinks of iniquity'*? The underlying cause needed to be examined. A not dissimilar debate is being carried on today.

A public meeting in April 1862 overwhelmingly carried a motion to petition Parliament for the Sunday closure of Public Houses. Later that year the magistrates received a petition calling for a reduction in the number of Public Houses, the signatories including seventeen clergymen. It was though very much business as usual. The magistrates renewed eighty-five licences, stood six over, and rejected only one.

*   *   *   *   *   *   *

Drink could induce strange fancies. A man taken into custody in Berwick delivered himself of the following.

> *'He told the man in charge of him that his wife was the Virgin Mary and that she had just been confined of a son. He prayed incessantly that his body might be covered with hair to keep him warm in winter and that his two attendants might be dressed by Heaven in Highland costume.'*

Its effect could also be terminal. Francis Dawson, landlord of The Cock and Lion in Bridge Street, enjoyed a night of convivial indulgence in Spittal. Attempting to return, he and a companion launched themselves on the river in a coble but lacked sail or oars. Dawson took off his jacket with the notion of holding it up to act as a sail, but, *'being unable to stand erect'* he plunged overboard. His companion, a Greenses fisherman, shouted loudly enough to be heard while clinging to the upturned boat and was rescued. Of Dawson though there was no trace.

SPITTAL INNS AND PUBLIC HOUSES 1806-1855

The seven directories that cover this period give these names and dates for houses and their landlords.

ESTABLISHMENT	1806	1822	1827	1834	1841	1847	1855
The South End	John Stafford						
The Golden Fleece	John Hall	William Hall	Wm. Hall	John Wood	James Ainslie	George Muers	George South
The Sheep	James Nesbit						
The Smack	Robert Thompson	Robert Wilson		John Swinhoe			
The Beehive	listed						
The Elephant		Thomas Spowart					
The Red Lion		Mark Edemson	Mark Edemson	Mark Edemson	Thomas Crowther	Thomas Crowther	Robert Alder
The Ship		Matthew Bell		James Wilson	James Wilson	Thomas Davidson	Robert McDougle
The Pitmans Arms		Mary Stafford	Mary Stafford		John Drysdale	John Drysdale	
The Sloop			Matthew Bell				
The Bell				William Wilson	William Wilson	Mary Moor	George Dawson
The King's Arms				Alexander Watt			Thomas Steel
The King's Head				Robert Wilson	Robert Wilson		Alexander Patterson
The Nag's Head				John Knox			
The Tweed Inn					William Smith	William Hogg	Thomas Crowther
The Commercial Inn						Henry Pickles	David Storar
The Coopers Arms						William Carr	George Carr
The Moulders Arms						Robert Hills	
The Salmon Inn						Thomas Brown	William Carr
The Blenheim Inn							John Purves
NO. OF LISTINGS	5	6	4	8	7	10	11

These dates of course give only an approximate idea of the span of an inn's existence or the length of a tenancy. Both are underestimated.

ORDINATION SERVICES
AT SPITTAL.

THE ORDINATION of Mr. WILLIAM PORTEOUS, as Colleague to the Rev. Mr. WHITEHOUSE, will take place in the UNITED PRESBYTERIAN CHURCH, SPITTAL, on TUESDAY the 16th of April 1850, at 11 o'Clock Forenoon, when the Sermon will be preached by the

Rev. Mr. WHITE of Wooler.

The ORDINATION PRAYER will be offered up by the

Rev. Mr. PORTEOUS, Coldstream.

The CHARGE to Mr. PORTEOUS, Jun., will be delivered by the

Rev. Mr HENDERSON, Coldingham.

And the Address to the Congregation will be given by the

Rev. Mr Glover, North Sunderland.

*** A Collection will be made at the End of the Services.

A FRUIT SOIREE

In connexion with the above Services, will be held the same Evening (Tuesday) in the Church at Spittal, when the following Gentlemen are expected to Address the Meeting :—

Rev. JAMES ANDERSON, Norham.	Rev. ADAM THOMSON, D.D., Coldstream.
„ DANIEL KERR, Dunse.	„ JOHN PEDEN, Berwick.
„ JAMES PORTEOUS, Coldstream.	„ PETER MEARNS, Coldstream.

Chair to be taken by the Rev. Mr. WHITEHOUSE at Half-past Six o'Clock Evening.

Charge for Admission, Sixpence each.
The Money to be taken at the Front Door of the Church.

On SABBATH, the 21st instant, the Rev. Mr. PORTEOUS will be introduced to his Congregation by the

REV. JAMES PORTEOUS OF COLDSTREAM,

Who will preach in the Morning; Service to commence at 11 o'Clock.

The Rev. Mr. PORTEOUS, Jun., will preach in the Afternoon;
Service to commence at 2 o'Clock.

The Rev. Mr. PORTEOUS, Coldstream, will preach again in the Evening;
Service to commence at 6 o'Clock.

*** Special Collections will be made at the End of each Service in aid of the Funds of the Congregation.

C. RICHARDSON, PRINTER, BERWICK.

14 The Church

To read about the Victorian Church is to visit an alien spiritual landscape where organised religion was the central and dominant influence in people's lives rather than the peripheral force it has now become. It was a time when it was advisable to pay a pew rent to be sure of your place in church; when the suspicion that a chaplain in Berwick Workhouse had Catholic leanings could remain a hot topic for months; when the Berwick Journal could publish a series of more than a dozen lengthy articles on the immortality of the soul and when its theological content regularly exceeded that of today's Church Times; when issues such as Puseyism and non-intrusionism, now the domain of scholars, were assumed to be of pressing concern to the general reader.

The religious message was not easily evaded. In Australia a Hawick gold-digger listened sceptically to a preaching minister, concluding that 'his message seems rather to clash with what we are here for' but gold-diggers clubbed together to buy a pulpit for Protestant ministers.

Yet the changes of the mid-Victorian era posed challenges to the church, in particular how much of the recently devised activity should be permitted on The Lord's Day. Should railways run? Should the Post Office open? Was it appropriate for people to wander round museums or listen to talks at such bodies as The Mechanics Institute?

The clergy turned out in force for key debates. During a public meeting in the Town Hall on the Post Office Alderman Johnstone complained that the theological context set by a series of clerical speeches made it hard for a layman to get a foothold in the debate. The meeting resolved on a petition to the House of Commons for Sunday closure, rapidly followed by a counter-petition against, though both were shortly after trumped by an Act of Parliament which enforced closure. There was controversy too over railway working, a public meeting in March 1848 voting 665-414 in favour of the Sunday running of trains. Here the clergy were more divided, some siding with the hard-line 'Askewites' who wanted a total shut-down but more inclined to press for restrictions. From its commencement though the Berwickshire Railway didn't run on Sundays.

Not that the clergy were always meekly deferred to. Debates on the Sunday opening of the museum and the Mechanics Institute were highly charged. The Rev. Dr. Cairns had spoken only four words in favour of closure before being interrupted by *'cheers, uproar, hisses, and cries of "sit down" '*. The solicitor R.B. Weatherhead argued powerfully that young men were far better off spending their leisure time on a Sunday in the Institute than in a public house. Both decisions though were in favour of closure. Yet the clergy would not have been able to prevail without a general climate of support.

* * * * * * *

In August 1852 the Rev. William Porteous held a service to mark the centenary of the ordination of the first Spittal minister. He reminded his congregation of the origin of their meeting house; of how Spittalers had been used to going to Berwick to worship but found themselves locked out during the height of the Jacobite frenzy in 1745.

This prompted the acquisition of an old malting house for services, after which the people were *supplied with sermon*. After a series of enlargements the Meeting House, occupying the same site as today's St. Paul's United Reform Church, could accommodate seven hundred and thirty people, being *neat and commodious*. It was given the bell placed on Spittal Point as a guide to fishermen on condition that that use be continued.

Spittal had ample time to get to know two of its clergymen, the Rev. William Whitehouse and the Rev. William Porteous whose consecutive ministries spanned sixty-five years. They appear to have carried on robustly without falling prey to the *nervous debility* which afflicted other clerics and required lengthy continental cures. Towards the end of his fraught ministry the Rev. G.F.Hamilton, Vicar of Berwick, gained the Bishop of Durham's permission to repair to the South of France for six months.

The Rev. William Whitehouse, who moved to Spittal after a spell at Thropton, wrote the trenchant analysis of Spittal's ills quoted from elsewhere. Unlike some other clerics he saw intemperance and other moral failings as a contributory rather than the root cause of Spittal's problems which he put down rather to the lack of economic opportunity and harsh social regulation. He spoke out when he saw the need. In a few lines of neat handwriting in blue ink he attacked what he saw as the dangerous scheme of the Greenwich railway. Some sixty now faded pencil signatures completed the petition to the Town Council. He tried to offer practical help, experimenting with the growing of potatoes to see if a way could be found to increase their yield. On his death, in October 1857, the Rev William Porteous took as his text for the funeral sermon *'Let me die the death of the righteous, and let my last end be like his'.*

By then the Rev. Porteous was well into his stride, having been the unanimous choice of the congregation in January 1850. For some years the two ministers worked in tandem: jointly, for example, attending Spittal School in order to conduct the annual examination.

Rather more is known of the Rev. William Porteous' activities as during his ministry local news became a more substantial feature of the newspapers. Billed at first as the Rev. Porteous (Jun.), his father being the Rev. James Porteous of Coldstream, he must have imbued the preoccupations of the Manse from an early age.

His preaching attracted favourable comment such as *very eloquent and impressive sermon*. Every January he delivered a sermon to the young. In 1853 he was reported to have addressed them *in a very interesting and impressive manner and seemed to keep up their attention to the close*. His text for 1855 was; *'O satisfy us early with thy mercy that we may rejoice and be glad all our days'*. After the service each child was given a copy of his address entitled *'This Glorious War'*, no doubt dealing with the restricted access to the Holy Places which was the ostensible cause of The Crimean War. Every year he took his Sabbath Class off on an excursion, usually to Duns during this period, later more often to Norham.

He took a strong interest in the broadening cultural life of Spittal, often chairing functions or arranging soirees, these as occasions either for adult discourse or juvenile treats. Keen to raise the musical standard he encouraged the introduction of psalmody by his precentor, Mr. Yeoman, whose choir had made sufficient progress by 1857 to put on a concert of sacred music. In the early 1860's William Jackson, the teacher, started training a flute band from the Sabbath Class, the players distinctively *'dressed in their picturesque blue guernseys and white trousers'*.

Appreciation was shown in a series of gifts such as a pulpit Bible and Psalter from his congregation and a gold ring from his Sabbath Class. Later the support and active participation that he was to get from the likes of the Herring Curers and Councillors, Boston and Edminson, greatly assisted with the building of St. Paul's.

The Rev. Dr. Cairns, whom Jackson mentions, was the dominant clerical presence in Berwick during this period. The first minister at Wallace Green, his preaching style permitted little wandering attention at the back. Senses were kept alert by *the majestic sweep of the arm, the emphatic tone of his voice, and the startling clap of his hands*. His sermons were very much a performance, the long, complex sentences reading less well in cold print.

Devoid of the airs and graces which were to mark some Anglican clergy later in the century there was respect for *his transcendent merits and abilities, which are heightened by the extreme modesty and childish simplicity of the man'.* Later for his amiability he was characterised as *'just a great big Newfoundland dog'* with *'a handshake like a vice - the only vice he has'.*

Interested in continental comparisons, he occasionally ventured abroad, being dismayed by French disregard of the Sabbath and congratulated by the King of Prussia on his excellent German. Other congregations attempted to lure him from Berwick to serve them but when he did finally leave Berwick it was to become Professor and later Principal at the Presbyterian College in Edinburgh.

*   *   *   *   *   *   *

From the mid-1850's there was a strong sense of living through a religious revival. The phrase was often used at the time. Much of it was of an evangelical nature though it seemed there were limits to fervour. *'No scenes of unwonted excitement, prostrations or striking down have been enacted in our streets or in our chapels'* noted The Berwick Journal.

The Primitive Methodists, who have been likened to early Socialists, were by now a familiar presence in Spittal. In August 1829 the missionary William Clough appeared in Spittal preceded by a boy with trencher and stick to rouse attention and preached to a sizeable crowd. The following year the first camp on Spittal Point was held and these continued for the next seventy-seven years. They quickly took on a substantial scale, an estimated two thousand people processing into the village from College Place in 1851 and saying prayers on the *'vacant ground in the centre of Spittal'.*

One strong supporter of the Primitive Methodists in their early Spittal years was John Alexander, Herring Curer. In a talk to their Sunday School he stressed the importance of temperance and suggested the formation of a juvenile teetotal society - an idea that certainly fell on fertile ground for a number of such societies were formed in the Borders. In 1851 a party of one hundred and eighty-seven from Berwick went on a juvenile teetotal demonstration in Edinburgh. Later that year a pleasure party from Kelso under the auspices of its juvenile teetotallers marched into Berwick preceded by the Duke of Roxburgh's Music Band.

The effect of a *'revival of religion during the winter months'* of 1860 was seen in a fisherman's soiree the following January which overflowed from the schoolroom to Andrew Morton's House. The Northumberland Coast Mission took a particular interest in fishermen.

There was too a substantial Anglican community which hoped one day to have its own church. A start was made in 1846 with a subscription of fifty pounds from the Durham Diocesan Church Building Fund. In January 1860 a room was made available for Divine Worship. It could hold about a hundred and fifty but a number were unable to get in. With continued fund raising, and a particular spurt in 1862, a total of £1667 had been reached by the following year by which time it was realistic to start looking at building plans.

* * * * * * *

In 1841 Bishop Jebb criticised the nature of much religious experience, remarking that *'early experiences are too often associated with gloom and constraint'*. For many though those words continued to describe the mood of the Sabbath. While the activities of a Sunday could bring comfort and a stirring of the soul to an adult, the child, as Jackson suggests, was more likely to be mightily relieved at its passing.

Yet religion too had its moments. In April 1859 the Baptists were at the centre of scenes of a *'tumultuous and uproarious description'*. They'd arranged to hold an Adult Baptism in a Spittal Herring Curing Yard. News of this event had though got around. Translated into secular terms this amounted to a spectacle of mass nudity and there were many happy so to perceive it.

> *'The villagers were somewhat anxious to witness the proceedings, consequently they collected in large numbers and used every effort to gain admission to the place; there was also a considerable number of persons collected from the northern side of the Borough, and the period selected for the service also happened to be that on which Mr. Porteous' congregation was dismissed from their afternoon service and whose chapel is immediately in front of the Herring House referred to. Altogether there was assembled on the streets an immense throng, who in consequence of various proceedings exhibited before them were soon in a state of the greatest excitement...... Eventually the crowd was got quit of.'*

15 Spittal Feast

The Spittal Feast never had the aura of the Tweedmouth Feast which got more Press coverage and attracted greater outside interest. Spittal participation was though a feature of the Tweedmouth celebration which included events such as the Spittal v Tweedmouth Foundry and pilot boat races. The first Monday in September was however the key date in the Spittal calendar.

Tradition had fixed the date of the Feast but the level of activity varied a good deal from year to year. Observers tended to note either too little spirit or too much. 1848 had seen *serious brawls and pugilistic encounters* but the following year was marked by a lack of *spirit and animation*. A poor herring fishing season could put a damper on things. Besides there being less money around crews were sometimes unwilling to give up a day's fishing with the season drawing to a close.

A series of Feasts from the mid-1850's seem to have been lively affairs. In 1856 there was *zeal and hilarity*. The following year despite salmon costing a shilling a pound – *a price never before heard of* – there was sufficient excitement for the police to intervene to suppress a Feast custom.

Tradition dictated that the drunkest man who could be found should be extracted from his Public House and dipped in the river. During this immersion he was proclaimed Mayor and his edicts were meant to hold sway during the remainder of the Feast. This kind of riotous spectacle was increasingly disapproved of by a now rather censorious society. The Town Police Clauses Act of 1847, a measure still regularly used today , required the prevention of public disorder. Jackson mentions fishermen recalling *that they could get drunk on boat-launchin' day without being taken to task for it*.

In 1858 there was a full programme of events. In addition to games on the beach there were:

River races for pilot cobles (25 shillings first prize)	*Climbing the greasy pole for a leg of mutton*
Foot races	*Sack race*
Running high leap	*Pole-leap*
Hop, step and leap	*Donkey races*

The jollity extended to the Tuesday when there were quoit matches. The presence of a number of strangers was remarked. The following year's event seems too to have been highly convivial, for *'the streets were thronged with people till a late hour'*. That year dancing was mentioned. Dancing at the Spa Well Green was to become a regular feature of later Feasts. Showmen were finding it worth their while to put in an appearance apparently doing a *'roaring trade'* among juveniles in 1861.

While the 1861 Feast had been noted for its *'good behaviour'* that of the following year was something of a low point in the history of the village.

The annual festival was commemorated on Sunday and Monday at Spittal. On entering the village on Monday evening, the first object that met the eye was a woman, in the last stages of helpless intoxication, lying upon the ground. She was accompanied by a child, probably about two years of age, and the cries of the poor infant attracted a crowd of persons to the spot. Plenty of abuse was directed against the poor unfortunate, but as she was unable to comprehend what was said to her, the onlookers might as well have held their tongues. One of the sympathisers with the child, unable to control her indignation, actually proceeded to inflict corporal chastisement upon the woman. Proceeding a little further up the village, a man might have been seen knocking down his wife's stall, scattering the bonbons, scrambling the ginger-bread, and then receiving a sound thrashing from his truly 'better half'. Turning to the right, here is a crowd, and going towards it, the visitor who is anxious to become acquainted with the manners and customs of the 'Spittallers', may see men, women, and children, all fighting 'at their own hand', as the Borderers used to say. Here is a woman ostensibly getting her husband or son out of the row, or shielding them from the blows of their opponents, but watch her, and you will see her deal that opponent a quiet blow with a force which could not be surpassed by those on whose behalf she was interfering. Occasionally, too, a knife might be seen – drawn, perhaps, more for the sake of bravado than with a view to its being used. Still the knife is a dangerous weapon in the hands of a drunken man, and its use cannot be too severely punished. One consoling matter about the Spittal folk is that no matter how seriously they may quarrel and fight at night, they are generally the best of friends next morning. Yet every one must regret the habits of drinking into which so many of the lower class there have fallen.'......'Taking the Feast altogether, we never saw more drunkenness and more fighting in Spittal at one time than we did on Monday evening. During the evening, one or two bands of music proceeded to the village, and promenaded the streets, playing lively airs.'

The omitted sentences proposed education rather than fewer licensed premises as the solution for excessive drinking. The Feast, which teetered on the edge of acceptibility by the 'respectable' classes, came under fire later in the 1860's when games and all other outdoor amusements were banned for a few years.

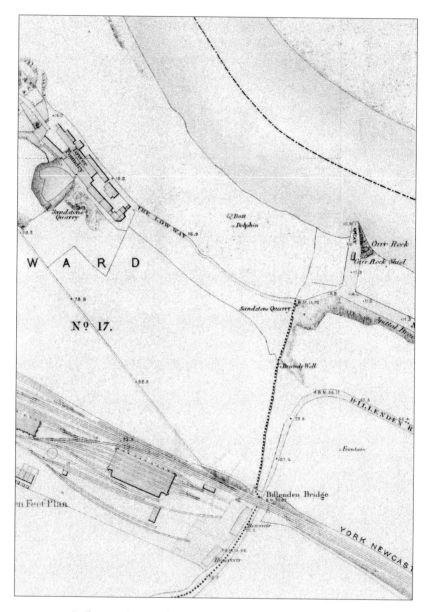

Railway, River and Road. Board of Health Map 1852

Section showing The Low Way, the rutted path to Berwick

16 The road to Berwick

Until 1835 Spittal was a part of North Durham, a situation which had certain advantages. It was possible to cock a snook at the Berwick authorities, particularly the police and the salmon-fishing guild, whose writ did not run south of the river. In that year though Spittal was politically linked with Berwick by the Municipal Corporations Act. In 1844 it was administratively connected.

Whether this union had been to Spittal's benefit many later doubted. The state of the roads served as a daily reminder of what was seen as neglect. Main Street had been macadamised to ease the passage of carts but was now full of pot-holes. But it was the state of the path from Spittal to the Tower Foundry at Tweedmouth that caused most agitation and prolonged exasperation.

Getting to Berwick had become less hazardous since the cutting back of the rockface at the Carr Rock in the 1840's. Before then the walker, if taking the coastal route, had been forced to scramble over rocks and seaweed at low tide. People were rumoured to have set off for Berwick never to be seen again.

By 1853 the footpath was in a 'dilapidated and obstructed condition, threatening the fracture of limbs to any unfortunate individual who may have occasion to cross from Spittal after daylight'. And accidents there were. An elderly lady fell over and broke her leg. So too did the ferry boatman, immobile until the gunboat crew heard his cries and carried him home. Then a *'young gallant'*, escorting his *'ladye love'* back from a trip to Auld Reekie, no doubt with more than footing on his mind, slipped near the narrowest part of the path into the *'muddy waters below'* dragging her with him. Both were able to scramble out. Poor lighting was to blame for some of these mishaps of which there were many more than reported. There was a general fear that plunging to the ground, especially after dark, would be taken as a sign of intoxication.

In March 1857 Cllr. James Wilson took the matter up in the Town Council. By September though the agreed Works Committee report had not materialised. Wilson was insistent. *'It ought to be repaired as it is in a very dangerous state.'*

The following year an irate *'native'* asked why the *'learned worthies of the bench'* regularly ignored petitions from Spittal but pressed ahead with improvements in their own areas. Complaints of casual and unfair treatment were becoming more insistent.

A public meeting in the Subscription School in February 1860 provided an outlet for frustration. In ten years the general rate had nearly quadrupled, from fourpence to fourteen pence, and what had they got for it? Why was expensive and unnecessary work taking place in Bridge Street when the Spittal path was still unrepaired ? Spittal with its Forge,Chemical Works, and three factories must be generating considerable revenue. *'What was become of their money?'* The Board of Health, the Town Council in another guise, was accused of *'a great neglect of their duties'.* Work was urgently needed on the sea wall which *'in many places was completely in ruins'.* It was resolved to send a deputation to the Town Council.

There were difficulties with the path not unlike those that have bedevilled the Point more recently. A number of parties were involved. Some of the land belonged to Mr. Greive of Ord who'd made known his opposition to any interference with his land. Another stretch was owned by Mr. Dickson of Alnwick who was not much more co-operative. More came under the control of the Harbour Commissioners. Assuming agreement could be reached between the parties who should bear the cost and in what proportion? Should the people of Spittal pay?

A few other things didn't help. Mr. Greive was frequently away and contact had to be made through his agent. When his attention was brought to focus on the path he asked for a map. Told he had already been given one he replied that *'he has not that by him'.* The Town Clerk had also lost his.

The Spittal deputation, consisting of Mr. James Wilson and Mr. John Burn, a joiner, were kept waiting outside while the Council deliberated. The Works Committee had finally got round to having a look, agreed that the path was dangerous, and that work was urgently needed, sea encroachment being the main problem. As for the long period of inactivity, the Mayor could only observe that *'the matter, through some means or other, was delayed'.* The effect of this was going to be that it would cost twice as much. He didn't really say why.

The Mayor did not though concede that Spittal had been getting less than its due. On the contrary, Berwick and Tweedmouth's accounts showed a surplus while Spittal's had a deficit. Mr. Wilson and Mr. Burn, when admitted, were clearly surprised to be told this. As they, and the Town Council, were merely told this by the Mayor after he'd been briefed by the Treasurer, no-one could look at the detail. The figures may well have been correct. Yet later when persistence yielded up accounts for scrutiny, oddities were found, mysterious hefty expenditure, and some blatant errors.

Agreement was finally reached. Mr. Greive was talked round, the Harbour Commissioners were to pay forty pounds and the people of Spittal thirty pounds. Work was to start straight away. Whatever was done though cannot have amounted to much. Two years later there were again calls for its repair. By the 1870's it was *no better than a ploughed field*. Not until 1881 did Spittal get the *good hard road* that many had confidently anticipated in the 1840's.

*   *   *   *   *   *   *

There was of course another route to Berwick. From June, 1838, a steam ferry became a familiar sight on The Tweed. It was owned and managed by Mr. James Wilson who named it *'The Queen'*. Thirty-five feet long and nine feet broad, she was judged capable of carrying thirty to forty passengers. She had too the useful asset in a river ferry of drawing only eighteen inches. She passed a *'river test'* with flying colours by sailing up The Tweed as far as the Whiteadder and covering the two miles in twenty minutes. Put into service she left Berwick on the hour, Spittal on the half-hour and started by charging twopence though this was halved the following year.

In January, 1849, however. the *Queen* was dragged from its moorings down an ice-covered Tweed, drifted out to sea, and was then cast on the beach as a wreck. This though did not interrupt the service for long for Mr. Wilson by then had a second boat undergoing almost finished repairs. He had too placed an order for a double-bowed boat to speed the landing process. This, the *'Mary and Jane'*, was launched in May 1849.

By 1860 the ferry landing was in poor repair, passengers having to flounder through a morass of mud at low tide. It continued to be *in a most shameful state* for some while. Operating during the herring fishing season could be tricky, the dense network of mooring ropes often leaving no option but to wait until boats put to sea. In 1863 the ferryman found himself entangled in a bureaucratic mesh when the Harbour Commissioners decided he needed a licence to work. This came with a number of bossy conditions. Hours of work were stipulated as was the fare (one penny). In effect they were turning him into their employee. Whatever its trials though, the ferry continued to be useful to Spittalers and popular with visitors.

Someone had a fringe benefit one May morning in 1846 when a six-inch trout leapt aboard the ferry during a crossing to Berwick. That afternoon a second did the same thing during a return to Spittal.

James Redpath

From the painting by L.D.McMorris

17 George Russell Jackson and the Redpaths

George Russell Jackson was born in 1844 and grew up in the north end, in that part of Spittal which had four public houses, three schools, several herring houses and an overpowering fishy smell. He was the second oldest of the six children of Thomas Jackson, Master Herring Curer, and his wife Ellen. Close by were the Ship Inn; the home of the veteran Herring Curer and temperance advocate John Alexander with his unusual household of five unmarried daughters, all in their twenties and thirties; and the homes of the schoolteacher George Boston, and the Herring Curer Thomas Crowther.

Some time during the 1850's Ellen Jackson was widowed and moved to 6, Albert Place where she took in lodgers. She may also have taken up her former craft of dressmaking to stay afloat. Here George would have become as familiar with the comings and goings of the summer visitors as he had earlier been with the business of herring curing.

A lively curiosity seems to have marked his youth. A pupil at the Subscription School he had more than a quick peep at two others, plainly being present during lessons. His account of the herring fishing relishes the detail and is coloured with the remembered awe of the experience of a youngster miles out in the German Ocean watching the buoys made from bullocks' bladders wash in the waves, listening to the men talk as they clustered round the fire in the sand-grate, and watching the ever-changing seascape. He had a keen eye for the quirks of his contemporaries. *'Noted Characters'* could only have been written by someone who'd found them intriguing.

Straitened family circumstances may have been a reason for his joining the army at the age of eighteen, serving for two years. The experience provided him with material for later sketches of army life, read with interest and approval by senior officers. In 1868 though he turned up in Boston, U.S.A., and went to work for someone he'd known since boyhood.

*   *   *   *   *   *   *

George Jackson wrote of the Subscription School as though both James Redpath and he were in it at the same time time. If so, they would have been at opposite ends of their school careers, Redpath being about ten years older.

Ninian Redpath has already been mentioned as the first teacher at the Subscription School and James was his eldest son. A man of great devoutness, indeed Jackson suggests an almost fanatical zeal, he dearly wanted James to become a minister. James though had other ideas and after leaving school he became a compositor on 'The Warder', a local paper which ran for most of the Victorian period, and roamed the Borders in search of stories. After the family emigrated to Michigan in 1850 he was resolved to become a journalist despite what his biographer suggests were heated discussions with his father. He got a job at Kalamazoo after camping on the doorstep of the absent editor for two days. While still a teenager he attracted the attention of the influential Horace Greeley and joined his New York Tribune paper.

This was the start of his career as a campaigning journalist. He was described as *'an energetic reformer - always seething with ardour in some cause or other, scornful of compromise, his enthusiasm giving interest and often brilliancy to his writing'.* His first great cause was the abolition of slavery which he advocated with such force as to become a marked man, carrying a gun and rousing his publishers' fears for his safety. During the civil war he reported from the Unionist side, on occasion swapping pen for pistol and leading guerilla raids. After the war he became involved in a project to form Haiti into a negro republic, becoming Haitian consul in Philadelphia, and was superintentent of schools in Charleston. His last great issue was that of Irish Home Rule. His presence in Ireland was sufficiently inflammatory for him to have to beat a hasty retreat to avoid arrest under the recently passed Coercion Act.

It was though for his lecture bureau that he was best remembered. This was a time when the public lecture was a regular feature of cultural life and the star lecturers Redpath attracted to his Boston Lyceum ensured large attendances. These included the philosopher Ralph Waldo Emerson and Mark Twain,some of whose surviving letters begin 'Dear Red'. Despite the large sums of money flowing in and out of the bureau Redpath was uninterested in money, and often hard up. He married late at fifty-five and died in 1891 after being run over in New York.

*   *   *   *   *   *   *

It was as the manager of a travelling Redpath bureau that George Jackson first gained a foothold in America. Journalism though was to be his line and he didn't stay there long.

He wrote for two papers and edited two others before joining 'The Somerville Journal'. It was while working for this little-known weekly paper that he established his reputation as a humorist and his witty pieces came to be widely republished throughout America. In 1884 he took his 'Pencillings' column to Boston after which he became known as 'The Funny Man of the Boston Courier' whose sayings were widely quoted from Maine to Texas.

He had a distinctive working habit. *'It is said by those who are intimate with him that not infrequently he will delay the preparation of his column for the Courier until a few hours before going to Press. Then he will seize the pen, and verse after verse, joke, squib, pun, all will roll from its nib, as water from an open tap.'*

His punning humour, a form then extremely popular, along with most of the genre seldom amuses today but his verse still has effect, as in –

THE GALL IN THE HONEY
"Oh, when does the honeymoon end, tell me, pray,
And the gall show itself in the honey?"
"The honeymoon ends, I believe, on the day
When the wife says she must have some money."

Sometimes the *'genial satirist'* could be a little acerbic.

THE WAY OF THE WORLD
He sows wild-oats, reforms, and he
Regains the place he held before;
She makes but one misstep and she
Is damned an outcast evermore.

Memoirs of one's youth are usually a product of old age but Jackson can have been barely thirty when he wrote 'A North Northumbrian Village' which proved popular. If some of the bracketed explanations of word meanings seem superfluous it needs to be remembered that he was writing for an American audience.

18 Spittal And Spittal Folks by George Russell Jackson

Extracts from *'A North Northumbrian Village'* first published in *'Atlanta Monthly'* around 1873.

They were reprinted by *'The Berwick Journal'* in 1883 and by popular demand appeared again the following year.

I HEBRON HILL

At the base of a hill, with the waters of the river Tweed lapping its northern and the waves of the German Ocean beating against its eastern side, lay the village. About a mile to the north, on the other side of the river, with its high walls and ruined castle, lay Berwick-upon-Tweed, famed in Border history and in Border song. To the west, high up on the sloping hills, gleaming in the summer sunshine and gently waving in the western breeze, were fields of yellow corn. Away to the south rugged rocks and frowning cliffs rose high into the air, a narrow strip of white sandy beach skirting their base. More distant in the same direction, the tall turrets of Holy Island Castle were clearly cut against the blue sky; near them, the ruins of the ancient abbey of Lindisfarne; and, farther distant still, the Fern Isles were scattered like dark specks on the shimmering surface of the German Ocean. Far away to the north, frowning darkly on the waters of the North Sea, rose St.Abb's head, – the proudest headland in Europe, – the dark waves tumbling themselves wrathfully against its jagged sides.

The village was an outlandish place, albeit, it was a favourite resort of the wealthy in summer; for its beach was regarded as one of the finest on the coast, affording facilities for bathing of which Newport could never boast. Consumptive dukes and superannuated duchesses might often be seen laving their aristocratic limbs in the waters which bleached its sands. There for a short season the famous Major Yelverton sojourned with his since discarded wife. There professors from the Edinburgh University and impecunious students from Durham Academy were wont to spend their hours of summer recreation, and there might be seen the country clergyman with a dozen of blooming daughters, the worn-out pedagogue from the base of the Cheviots, the coal-merchant from Newcastle, and the weaver from Paisley. But these were only transient visitors; they had nothing in common with the inhabitants; they lived in a different world. The visitors were members of society; the inhabitants belonged to the village.

In his next article Jackson characterised the inhabitants, described two red-letter days in the fishing calendar and the delights of the herring fishing.

II THE INHABITANTS

It would be difficult to find in any other part of the civilised world a class of people exhibiting so many peculiarities of character, so much ignorance combined with the highest order of intelligence, so much piety combined with the most daring profanity, as was to be found in this little village. Most of the inhabitants were fishermen, – rough, uncouth men as rugged as the rocks which raised their frowning fronts in defiance of the North Sea waves. Men, the greatest number of whom had never seen the inside of a schoolhouse, and who listened to the call of a church bell only when it was rung in foggy weather to guide them in safety to their harbour. They believed the great end of life consisted in catching as many fish as possible, and, believing this, they pursued their calling with zeal. Two or three hours before sunrise every morning, when the condition of the weather permitted, they launched their cockle-shell craft and sped miles away into the ocean.

* * * * * * *

About the beginning of July the herring season commenced; and great were the preparations that were made for it. An entire day was devoted by the fishermen to launching the boats. This day was called 'boat launchin' doon day' and on the close of the herring season another day was devoted to dragging the boats up on to the banks. This was called 'boat launchin' up day'. These were not ordinary days. They were to the villagers what the Fourth of July is to Americans; looked forward to for months.

The owner of each boat paid seven shillings and sixpence for launching. There were twenty-eight boats, which made a sum total of ten pounds ten shillings. This was distributed among the landlords of the thirteen public-houses in the village, and after the boats were all launched men and boys repaired to the Public-houses, when the 'boat launchin' spree' commenced. About ten o'clock on the night of boat-launchin' day' fighting began, rather mildly at first, but as the night wore on the strife increased. Then were heard fearful oaths and imprecations, wild shouts and startling cries. All the fishermen, with a few exceptions, were drunk. The village was in an uproar. Suddenly the door of a public-house would be thrown open, a glare of light streaming into the street, and a drunken crowd would issue forth. In a few moments a circle was formed, in the centre of which a couple of fishermen were to decide which was the better man.

"Are ye ready?" was asked in a fierce tone by one.

"Ay; are ee ?" from the other.

"Take that, ye cowart (coward). I'll batter ye, ye loosey thief."

Fierce now became the strife, the surrounding crowd urging on the combatants to deeds that would render them famous in the annals of 'boat launchin' days'.

"Go in t' 'im Jimmy." – "Hammer 'im Jack." – "Gie 'im a cross-ballicker"(that is, knock him down and strike him as he falls). – "Stap that. Jack; it's nae fair strikin' 'im when he's doon." – "Fair play. He's no gittin' fair play; bit I'll see that he gits it," shouts a friend of the prostrate gladiator, springing into the ring.

This was the signal for a general engagement, and in a few moments the entire crowd, men, women, and children, were fighting. All order was lost. Friends knocked down friends, husbands beat their own wives, and wives tore the hair from the heads of their own husbands. Blood flowed, eyes were closed for indefinite periods,shirts and shawls were torn to shreds, and red night cowls trampled in the dust. When the crowd became exhausted they separated peacefully, and met each other as friendly as ever on the following day, all the differences buried until Spittal Feast or next 'boat launchin' day.'

*   *   *   *   *   *   *

In this part of the world and on the ocean the moonlights are perfectly beautiful, so bright yet so soft, – so tender, so subdued. Nor were the ignorant, uncouth fishermen insensible to the charm of such a spectacle. Clustered around the fire blazing brightly in a grate which was secured in a wooden box, – the bottom being covered in sand about two inches in depth to prevent its ignition from the frequently falling embers, – they gazed around them with feelings akin to awe, and drank in the beauty of the scene which lay before them, stretching away north, south,east, and west as far as the eye could reach; with such expressions as "Dysn't she look bonnie the night!" referring to the moon; or, "Wull, it's worth lossin' sleep t'see sic a thing as this!" referring to the scene. Thirty miles distant to the north the light on St. Abb's Head gleamed brightly, and twenty miles to the south the revolving lights of the Fern Islands shot their rays far out on the ocean. Westward rose the Cheviots and the Lammermuirs, and eastward, shimmering in the soft moonlight until they met the sky, stretched the waters of the German Ocean. There lay a delighted gaze. Even more beautiful and more impossible of description was the spectacle presented when the fishermen began the task of hauling in their nets. The fish in the nets, as they passed over the side of the boat dripping with phosphorescence, gleamed with auroral brilliancy, and it seemed as if the fishermen had been fishing in the sky and had caught a sheet of the Northern Lights.

*　　*　　*　　*　　*　　*　　*

III FACILITIES FOR EDUCATION

There were three schools in the village: 'the subscription school' and two private schools. The subscription school was supported by voluntary subscriptions, that is, those of the villagers who were interested in promoting the means of education subscribed money for the purchase of books and other material necessary for the school. The salary of the master was seventy pounds a year and a free house. A school fee of twopence a week was paid by scholars over six years of age, and a penny per week under that age. These fees went towards the payment of the master's salary, the remainder being made up by subsciption.

Arithmetic, grammar, geography, and sacred history were the chief studies. The scholars were also taught to sing – not by note, but by ear. The master of the subscription school was a kind-hearted, but stern and scrupulously conscientious man – well educated, but full of that spirit of piety, almost amounting to fanaticism, which is peculiar to the Border character. The school opened in the morning with the singing of a hymn and the reading of a chapter from the Bible, which the master expounded as he read. After finishing the reading of the chapter, the master invoked the Divine blessing on the exercises of the day. With closed eyes and folded hands the scholars knelt in silence, while the master, with uplifted face, and solemn aspect, returned thanks for past mercies and supplicated strength and wisdom in discharging the solemn duty of impartial instruction to the young. It was a beautiful sight – nearly three hundred boys and girls, varying in age from four to fifteen years, some in rags. some clothed neatly and respectably, some with begrimed faces and unkempt hair, some clean, rosy, and fresh, their hair smoothly combed and their clothing neat and comfortable, kneeling before their unpainted, unvarnished pine desks, silent and with closed eyes, the master, his face glowing with the inspiration of faith, with uplifted eyes solemnly invoking the blessing of God on his labours, and the young committed to his charge.

Truly 'from scenes like these auld Scotia's grandeur springs,' as much as from the scenes so beautifully described by the Ayrshire ploughman. Prayer finished, another hymn was sung, after which the scholars applied themselves to their different tasks. The scholars were divided into eight classes, according to the degree of proficiency they had attained. The classes were composed of boys and girls indiscriminately, and it was no unusual thing to see a girl at the head of the class. The master taught the first class and appointed tasks for the remainder, a scholar of the first class taught the second class and the teachers for the remaining classes were taken from the second class. These teachers were changed every day. The master, albeit kind and benevolent, was a rigid disciplinarian, and his school was a model of order. He turned out some excellent scholars, many of whom could be pointed out today, holding high positions in the literary and commercial world. His own son,who was educated in the school, and received no greater advantages than were afforded the son of the poorest and most ignorant fisherman of the village, occupies a high place in the ranks of American journalism; and it is worthy of remark that other graduates of his school are rapidly rising to conspicuous positions in the same profession.

The private schools were kept, one by an old man familiarly known in the village as Dominie Bowson. and another by a woman named Esther Lauther. These were regarded as primary schools although the dominie pretended to run in opposition to the subscription school. The dominie was very proud of his scholastic accomplishments, which consisted of a knowlege of arithmetic and geography. He did not pretend to teach grammar, affirming it as his opinion that it was a useless accomplishment. "Feegurs," said he, "Feegurs is the thing. Learn a youngster feegurs, an' he's a' right." The more intelligent fathers of families did not endorse the dominie's philosophy, and sent their children to the subscription school. The dominie had, nevertheless, quite a number of scholars of all ages and both sexes, many of whom turned out creditably. Being lame from an accident – he had been a coal miner – and confined to his chair, his pupils not infrequently opposed his authority. He kept upon his desk a cat-o'-nine-tails, denominated the 'tawse'; this he would throw to a misbehaving scholar, who would bring them to the dominie and stand until he received a thrashing commensurate with the offence. Some of the bolder scholars would refuse to take the hint thrown out by the dominie with the tawse, and allow the corrective agent to lie beside them unnoticed. This indifference would arouse the dominie's wrath and he would deliver himself as follows:-

"Ho, ho! So ye won't bring them, won't ye? Ho, ho, ha, ha! We'll see if you won't, ye jackass; ye – ye – ye what-ye-may- call-it; ye jackynapps; ye nint' feegur without the tail (a cipher). I'll wallop ye, ye fisher's brat, I'll be whuppit (whipped) if I don't. I'll make the red ink (blood) fly, ye what-ye-may-cal1-it !"

During the delivery of this extemporaneous threatening address, the exasperated dominie raised his hand to a level with his eye, the index finger pointed like a pistol at the rebellious and, too often, indifferent pupil. His passion spent, he would sink back in his chair and resume his wonted serene demeanour.

Miss Esther Lauder's school was attended principally by girls, who were taught arithmetic, the alphabet, and plain sowing, darning and knitting. Besides these there was Hobbie Elliott's school, which, from the peculiarity of the studies pursued in it, deserves special mention.

Hobbie Elliott was a fisherman who had seven sons. Having no faith in schools, he determined to educate his sons himself. He could neither read nor write; but, as he said himself, he had got on in the world without those accomplishments. He was prosperous; the majority of educated men in the village were not so comfortable as he, which fact was unquestionably owing to their knowledge. His sons should never be ruined by a schoolmaster. "Na, na," he concluded, "I'll school them masel'."

*   *   *   *   *   *   *

The villagers believed that the factual account of disasters given in the newspapers left something out.

IV SUPERSTITIONS

At one time in the history of the village all the fishermen, with the exception of one boat's crew,were lost in a storm. It was during the winter season, while they pursued the haddock and cod fishing. About an hour before dawn, when the fishermen were preparing to go to sea, a woman, tall, and clad in a white dress and black shawl, was observed to go down on to the beach and touch every boat as she passed it, except one, with her hand. All the boats went to sea except the one that she had not touched, – two of her crew were sick. About an hour after sunrise a storm arose, such a storm as had never been seen on that coast. In a few minutes the sea ran mountains high, and not one of the boats, nor a solitary man out of all their crews, ever reached the shore. They were all drowned. It was a terrible calamity and almost depopulated the village.

On another occasion, as the boats were going out, a woman stood on the beach and shook her hand at one of them. That boat never returned. On approaching the harbour a thick fog settled down, she struck on a rock, and her crew, which consisted of four brothers, were drowned.

✲   ✲   ✲   ✲   ✲   ✲   ✲

No death had occurred in the village since its foundation but had been 'forewarned', so the old women said. On 'the night that Widow Ruffel's bairn died', a pig, with its throat cut, had been seen to walk across the kitchen floor and disappear beneath the hearth stone. And the 'night that auld Tam Crystal died, a black cat cam doon the chimley an' walked out at the door'. When old Jemmy Benney was in his last sickness, a strange man was seen at midnight standing near the door of the house, with a bloody razor in his hand. Next morning Jemmy was dead. 'Jack Johnson's dog growled a' night when Tammy Rutherford died', and on the night that the Lapwing was lost, with all hands, a woman with dishevelled hair was seen on the beach just before dark, wringing her hands and weeping.

While not typical, the village had its religious fanatics. Jackson describes the child's dread of the Sabbath and the restraint it imposed on adults.

V RELIGION

The population of the village was about eighteen hundred; most of them were fishermen. A few mechanics, four or five fish-merchants, and some persons with hereditary incomes of from fifty to seventy-five pounds a year, who were called independent, composed the aristocracy. The majority of the aristocracy professed religion, and attended 'meetings' on Sundays. Out of the entire number of fishermen only five or six were conspicuous for their piety; but these were very remarkable men when viewed in comparison with their professional brethren. There was only one house of worship in the village, and this was of the Presbyterian denomination. Strange to say, not one of the pious fishermen belonged to it. Two were Baptists, one a Swedenborgian, one an Irvingite, and one stood alone, calling himself a member of the church of Christ.

In the families of these men, as may be imagined, religious discipline was very rigid. The Sabbath was most strictly observed. The food for Sunday was cooked on Saturday afternoons and eaten cold on the following day. The children were not allowed to go beyond the threshold of the door, unless to church or Sunday School. In the house they were not allowed to indulge in the luxury of leaning back in their chairs, unless they were reading the Bible, Doddridge's Rise and Progress, The Pilgrim's Progress, Paley's Theology, or Harvey's Meditations Among the Tombs. The children of the family, from the eldest down to the boy or girl of three or four years old, were each obliged to commit to memory a chapter, or portion of a chapter, from the Old or New Testament during their leisure moments on Sunday, and repeat it without the book after family worship in the evening. The parents fully agreed with Dr. Watts that "Satan finds some mischief still for idle hands to do," and the children were kept busy. The severity of this discipline frequently had the effect of engendering a hatred in the minds of the less religiously inclined children against every form of piety, and runaways from the parental authority to the large sea-ports of Newcastle-on-Tyne and Shields – where the boys bound themselves as apprentices in merchants' vessels, – were not uncommon.

Among the members of the Presbyterian church, with a few exceptions, the young were not ruled so rigidly. The children were allowed to lean back in their chairs, and I dare say the circumstance is yet fresh in the mind of every inhabitant of the village of a boy caught one Sunday afternoon in the act of impaling a fly on a needle, who only received a slight whipping on the following day. No thrashing was done on Sunday. Crimes perpetrated on Sunday were not punished on that day, and the children who would otherwise have joyfully hailed the approach of Monday frequently awaited its arrival in terror.

* * * * * * *

The Presbyterians observed the ordinance of the last supper four times a year, once every three months. One Saturday evening, two women got into a dispute. They were both members of the church, and the following day – Sunday – was 'sacrament day'. The dispute ran high, and harsh words were used. At length one of the women, her face inflamed with anger, stalked up to the other, and, shaking her clenched fist before the eyes of her antagonist, shouted wrathfully, -

"Ye hussy, if it hadna been Sacrament Sunday th' morn, I'd a walloped ye !"

The children of the fishermen were, as I have already stated, obliged to gather bait, and had no opportunity of attending school regularly, even if their parents were willing that they should. Some of them attended Sunday School, where they learned the child's catechism and sometimes portions of scripture. It was no uncommon thing to find children, who had not learned the alphabet, able to repeat the catechism from beginning to end, and whole chapters from the Bible. The son of a fisherman, who had never seen the inside of a day school or Sunday School, one Sunday morning found himself clad in a new suit of corduroy, made by Tam Carr, the tailor of the village in the primary class of the Sabbath-school. The teacher, an elder of the church, asked the boy if he had been to school before. The boy answered "No."

"Who made you ?" interrogated the teacher.

The boy, his mind filled with thoughts of his new suit of corduroy, promptly answered , -

"Tam Carr, bit they're no' paid fur yet."

VI NOTED CHARACTERS

I have already mentioned the jetty corner. This was a piece of common situated near the edge of the river where a small landing, for the ferryboats which plied between the village and Berwick-on-Tweed, ran out. It was the custom of the old men of the village to meet at this place and indulge in the latest gossip. It was also the debating ground. All disputes that were found impossible of settlement by physical means were brought to the jetty corner and submitted to the patriarchs for settlement. Debate often ran high, and it was not uncommon to hear one disparaging the character of another. Although it might be called the village parliament, no order was observed in conducting debate. All the members spoke at once, and gave their opinions in the same breath. At such times, the by-stander could not hope to understand a word of what was being spoken. The patriarchs themselves did not understand each other. The debate went on, nevertheless.

Some of these old men were peculiar characters. Old and feeble they were, but each one had a strongly marked individuality. One (Joe Steele) bore the reputation of having been the greatest liar in the village, and, though age had dimmed his eyes, it had not impaired his inventive faculty. Standing with one foot in the grave, he could tell a lie, at which Munchausen would have shuddered, with as much satisfaction and as earnestly as when he was in full possession of his strength. Village boys, in giving each other the lie, would say: "That's ane o' Joe Steele's figgers." Another (Jamie Smith) was noted as the laziest man in the village, and nobly he sustained his reputation. Labour he regarded with the greatest aversion. He was too lazy to go to bed, and, after he got to bed, too lazy to get up. Nothing but the pangs of hunger could induce him to exert himself to eat, and after eating he wished he would remain satisfied for ever. His peculiarity was visible in his dress. Each garment was fastened with only one button. He had no laces in his shoes. "What's the use," said he, "of havin' show laces; if ye fas'n them i' the mornin' ye have t' loos'n them again at night." The only subject in which he appeared to take an interest was that of new inventions. He looked forward to the time when men "wadna need t' have buttons on their claes, and when chairs wi' soft cushions wud be placed at street corners."

Another, and the most striking, character was William Johnson, familiarly known as au'd Wull Johnson. He was a very old man, nearly ninety but strong and vigorous. He was the champion debater of the 'outs' of the assembly. He always differed from everybody, and in his own belief he was always right. He never formed an opinion until everybody else had formed his; then, after all had delivered themselves, he would take a position in direct antagonism to each, and he always triumphed, no matter how numerous and how strong the majority. And how he enjoyed his triumphs! How he would chuckle and mutter to himself, "Beat them again, the d----d fyells."

There came a day, however, when the champion disputant was to be vanquished. Alas that such a day should ever have dawned !

An old and much respected woman, long known in the village for her kindness and benevolent disposition, went the way of all the living, and her funeral was attended by the assembly in a body. A few of the patriarchs, among them Wull Johnson, stood at the grave and watched the coffin – a plain pine on the lid of which a small metal plate bore the dates of her birth and death and her age – slowly lowered, and the earth placed upon it.

On the following day the assembly met early to discuss the probable chances of the deceased reaching heaven. Contrary to his usual custom, Wull Johnson coincided in the opinion of the others that "she was a'right." But shortly after, when the question of her age came up, Wull affirmed that the others had mistaken the figures on the coffin-plate. He had carefully scrutinised them – indeed he attended the funeral for that purpose – and the woman was not so old, by five years, as the others stated. The others had also seen the figures on the coffin-plate, and they were certain that Wull Johnson was wrong.

"The wumman was seeventy," said Joe Steele.

"Ye're a liar," replied Wull Johnson; "she was only sixty-five."

"I saw the feegurs," said Joe Steele, mildly.

"Feegurs! what d' ye ken aboot feegurs! where did ye learn feegurs ? ye're as ignorant as a cuddy"(ass).

"Never mind, the wumman was seeventy year au'd."

Wull Johnson flew into a terrible passion; the other members sided with Steele. As usual, Wull himself, unaided and alone, represented the minority, and he braced himself for the contest. From morn till noon they argued, from noon till dewy eve. Wull Johnson would not budge an inch. The assembly did not adjourn for tea, but continued the debate, and midnight found them exhausted, but as far from settlement as ever. At last Joe Steele proposed that the assembly should proceed to the grave-yard, disinter the coffin, examine the dates on the plate, and fill in the grave again. The proposition was favourably received, and provided with spades, the patriarchs tremblingly took their way to the grave-yard. Stationing a sentinel at the gate, they proceeded to the grave, and in a short time the coffin-lid was laid bare. A match was lighted, and the figures on the plate were revealed to the gaze of all.

Wull Johnson was wrong!

Chuckling with glee the triumphant patriarchs filled up the grave, and when the last shovelful of earth had been thrown upon the mound, Joe Steele, with a smile of triumph, turned to Wull Johnson and in an exulting tone said, -

"Weel, Wull, what have ye t' say now, eh? Ye've seen the feegurs, an' they are jest as we said."

"Oh! ye ignorant anes, ye shuckle-heads, yes, I've seen the feegurs, **but the feegurs have been changed since I saw them afore !**"

"What! wha cud change them since yesterday an' the coffin i' the grave ?"

"I dinna ken, nor I dinna care. Bit they have been changed."

A general laugh drove Wull from the grave-yard. He did not make his appearance at the jetty-corner next day. His spirit was crushed. He never held up his head again, and, when the doctor told him he was dying, he could only murmur, "Ye're a liar," and, without continuing the argument, breathed his last. After Wull's death the assembly was broken up. Where they all agreed, it was impossible to get up a dispute. Joe Steele for some time drew them together by relating his marvellous adventures, but they tired of these at last; and six months after Wull's death, the jetty corner was deserted by all save lazy Jamie Smith, who dragged himself to the old rendezvous every morning – too lazy to change his old habits – and lay sleeping until carried home by his son at night. The patriarchs have been gathered to their fathers, and the village, which now boasts an Episcopal as well as a Presbyterian church, is being educated and otherwise improved.

But the fishermen still think, with a sigh, of the good old days when they drank gin at every meal, and could get drunk on "boat-launchin' day' without being taken to task for it.